JOYFUL, PATIENT, FAITHFUL

Jenifer Metzger

JOYFUL, PATIENT, FAITHFUL

A 90-Day Devotional Book for Mom

Illustrations by
Alessandra De Cristofaro

ROCKRIDGE
PRESS

TO MY HUSBAND

Jeremy, thank you for your
endless love and support.

I love you always and forever.

TO MY CHILDREN

L(J), J(B), G, and Z, you are my
sweet blessings from heaven.

I am honored to be your mom.

A special dedication to my firstborn baby, who
as I type this is preparing for her firstborn baby.
Sissy, motherhood is an adventure. Lean on God,
and the adventure will always be blessed.

CONTENTS

Introduction   1

Day 1: Blossom in Motherhood 4

Day 2: You Are Chosen 6

Day 3: You Are Beautiful 8

Day 4: Knitting the Perfect You 10

Day 5: Replenish Your Oxygen 12

Day 6: Thanks for the Same Old, Same Old 14

Day 7: Mission Possible 16

Day 8: Trust the Father 18

Day 9: Savor the Status Quo 20

Day 10: Use God's Measuring Stick 22

Day 11: Living the Fruits 24

Day 12: Love: Be Love 26

Day 13: Joy: Search for It in Blessings 28

Day 14: Peace: God Is Your Kids' Chaperone 30

Day 15: Patience: A Fruit and a Vine 32

Day 16: Kindness: A Little Goes a Long Way 34

Day 17: Goodness: Be Good Because He Is Good 36

Day 18: Faithfulness: You Gotta Have Faith 38

Day 19: Gentleness: A Gentle Touch Means So Much.... 40

Day 20: Self-Control: Is It Even Possible? 42

Day 21: Lessons from a Crepe Myrtle 44

Day 22: His Power Is Empowering 46

Day 23: Discipline versus Punishment 48

Day 24: Mom, Take Two 50

Day 25: Kids Need the Bible, Too 52

Day 26: Hope Springs Eternal 54

Day 27: A New Day, A New Gift 56

Day 28: Say His Name 58

Day 29: A Sweet-Smelling Fragrance 60

Day 30: Overworked. Underappreciated 62

Day 31: Lean on Jesus 64

Day 32: Hello, My Name Is Jenifer and I Am a Yeller 66

Day 33: Enjoy the Season 68

Day 34: Do unto Others 70

Day 35: The Original Artist 72

Day 36: Time to Spring Clean 74

Day 37: Trust Fall 76

Day 38: Don't Lose Yourself 78

Day 39: Mom, Take Care of Yourself 80

Day 40: Hanging in the Balance 82

Day 41: Connect with Your Child 84

Day 42: Setting the Spiritual Tone of Your Home 86

Day 43: Child Pray 88

Day 44: Church Beyond the Pews 90

Day 45: She Struggles, Too 92

Day 46: Find Your Mama Team 94

Day 47: Making Memories 96

Day 48: Speak Life 98

Day 49: Winning the War 100

Day 50: Team Family 102

Day 51: Remembering Your Value 104

Day 52: Limits Make Us Limitless 106

Day 53: Are You Brokenhearted? He Is Near. 108

Day 54: Whatever It Takes 110

Day 55: Allow Help 112

Day 56: Use the Manual 114

Day 57: "Yes" Means "Yes" and "No" Means "No" 116

Day 58: They're Always Watching! 118

Day 59: Even Jesus Had Family Dinner 120

Day 60: Who Are You Really? 122

Day 61: Rip Off the Label 124

Day 62: We Belong to Him 126

Day 63: Love All Your Neighbors 128

Day 64: Your Win Is My Win 130

Day 65: God's Protection 132

Day 66: Get Ahold of Yourself 134

Day 67: Wear Your Armor 136

Day 68: Give Credit Where Credit Is Due 138

Day 69: Quieting the Noise 140

Day 70: When Depression Takes Over 142

Day 71: Balancing Mary and Martha 144

Day 72: Moms Unite 146

Day 73: Jesus Isn't Lost 148

Day 74: It Takes Perspective 150

Day 75: Sweep Your Heart 152

Day 76: Paralyzed by Indecision 154

Day 77: Your Child's Personal Trainer 156

Day 78: Are You Full of Praise? 158

Day 79: Be Hungry 160

Day 80: Getting There, but Not Quite There Yet 162

Day 81: Tune In to the Right Voice 164

Day 82: Don't Just Phone It In 166

Day 83: Keeper of the Home 168

Day 84: Exercise Your Spiritual Muscles 170

Day 85: His Faithful Love 172

Day 86: Give Him a Call 174

Day 87: Guilt-Free 176

Day 88: Our Teacher 178

Day 89: Ordinary Is Extraordinary 180

Day 90: Mama Needs ~~Coffee Chocolate Wine~~ Jesus . . . 182

Conclusion 184

References 186

Welcome to *Joyful, Patient, Faithful!* I am thrilled that I will be a small part of your day over the next three months. Before we begin, I want to share why this devotional is so important to me. I grew up in the church and was saved at a young age. In my early teens, I renewed my relationship with God as I came to know Him as my own Savior, and not just by living through my parents' relationship to faith. I loved reading the Bible and journaling. By the time I was 16, I had read through the Bible several times (if you were in Missionettes as a girl, you get it!) and had memorized countless verses.

My husband and I married when I was just 17. Yes, you read that right. *Seventeen.* By the time I was 22, I had four small kids. As you can imagine, being a young mom of four kids under the age of five, life was crazy. Beautiful. Wonderful. Amazing. But crazy.

The busyness of everyday life soon took over and I forgot the joy and beauty, not to mention the necessity, of spending time with Jesus each day. Before long, my Bible became nothing more than a Sunday-morning accessory.

Fast-forward a few years, when I could feel the neglect. My soul yearned for *something*. While my life was wonderful—an amazing husband, incredible children, beautiful home, wonderful family, great church, everything I could ask for—I felt empty. I finally realized what was lacking and put in the effort to get it back: my time with Jesus. My desire is to help you navigate the everyday busyness of life and motherhood, and find your way back to the Word, too.

For each of the next 90 days, in a single season, we will delve into God's Word, share in a devotion, pray together, and end with a thought-provoking question or task to help you dig deeper. My hope is that you fellow busy moms will use this book as a time-friendly way to connect with God over the next three months. And use it as a keepsake to which you can refer time after time, season after season, when motherhood becomes challenging or you need some support, compassion, or an opportunity to connect with your faith.

So, my friend, as we journey through the next three months, I pray that you will develop a deep love for the Bible, learn how to carve out time to spend with Jesus each day, and feel supported knowing that you aren't in this alone. Let's begin!

Blossom in Motherhood

Your word is a lamp for my feet
and a light on my path.

Psalm 119:105 (CSB)

I love flowers and plants of any kind. I do not have a green thumb, however. I'm actually more of a plant killer. Yet, one summer, my husband decided to surprise me with two beautiful, large, hanging flowerpots. With my history, I feared that in less than a week they would be dead. But when I found out the price he paid, I knew I had to try my best to follow the nursery's instructions: *Water twice a day. Give six to eight hours of sun. Fertilize once a week.* Okay, I can do this.

I am proud to say I kept the flowers alive all summer long. Why did these flowers live and thrive when I had killed dozens of others? Because I watered them twice every day, I left them in the sun, and I fertilized them once a week.

While admiring my flowers, I felt God nudge my heart. *That is all it takes. Spend time with Me every single day. Look for the Son throughout the day. Go to church and spend time worshipping with other believers every week.* If I don't water my flowers every day, they will shrivel up and die. If I don't spend time with God every day, my spirit will shrivel up. If you are feeling dry, lost, and lonely, stop and think. Have you spent time with God today? Have you looked for the Son today? Make spending daily time with God a priority and see how you blossom. When you blossom, you will see your journey in motherhood blossom as well.

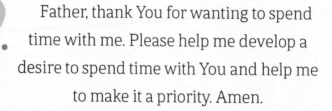

Father, thank You for wanting to spend time with me. Please help me develop a desire to spend time with You and help me to make it a priority. Amen.

♦ Make a concrete plan that works for you to spend intentional time with Jesus each day.

♦ Continue to pray, asking God to help you desire time with Him.

SHARE YOUR THOUGHTS: _____

_____

_____

_____

_____

_____

_____

_____

_____

_____

_____

_____

_____

You Are Chosen

For we know, brothers and sisters loved by God,
that He has chosen you.

1 Thessalonians 1:4 (CSB)

I wish that I could sit down with you right now. I'd offer you a glass of sweet tea and a chocolate chip cookie fresh from the oven. I'd look you in the eye, and I'd make sure you were looking back. I would tell you gently but firmly that *you are chosen.*

This journey of motherhood can make us forget this simple fact. Motherhood is equal parts beautiful and hard. We question every decision we make. We wonder if we are doing a good enough job or if our children are doomed. Breast or bottle? Cloth diaper or disposable? Too much screen time? Too many sweets? Homeschool or in-person school?

In the face of all this uncertainty, you need to remember that God hand-picked you to be the mother to your children. Whether you are worried about everyday decisions or are facing hardships with a child, God knew you were the right fit to be their mom. When you come to this realization that God has chosen you to be the mother of your children, you are empowered to walk this journey of motherhood. He is there to equip you and walk beside you.

Father, thank You for choosing me.
Thank You for handpicking me to be a mom.
Please equip me to raise my children
according to Your Word and walk beside
me on this path. Amen.

♦ Today, give yourself grace.

♦ Tell your child that you are happy God chose you to be their mom.

SHARE YOUR THOUGHTS: _____

_____

_____

_____

_____

_____

_____

_____

_____

_____

_____

_____

_____

DAY 3

You Are Beautiful

So God created man in His own image;
He created him in the image of God;
He created them male and female.

Genesis 1:27 (CSB)

Friend, hear my words loud and clear: You are beautiful. Even with dark circles under your eyes from lack of sleep, spit-up on your shirt, or gray hairs peeking out, you are beautiful.

You, yes *you*, were created to look like God. He created you exactly the way He wanted you. He gave you the nose He wanted you to have. He shaped your eyes and colored them exactly as He wanted. He decided if you would be tall or short. You were made in His image.

We can be so critical of ourselves. My hair is too curly. Too straight. I'm too tall. Too short. And our weight, oh, our weight! If you could see me now, I am offering up a big eye roll. It's hard to watch television or look at a magazine without feeling "less than." We already have so much pressure on us as moms that striving to look "perfect" adds an unnecessary and unrealistic burden we don't need.

We forget that we were created to look like our loving Father and that He loves and wants us exactly the way we are. We are special and important to Him. We—you—are God's masterpiece.

Father, thank You for creating me.
Thank You for wanting me and loving me
exactly the way I am. Help me see the beauty
that You created and learn to love myself as
You love me. Amen.

♦ Today, when you look in the mirror, don't sigh, don't cry, and don't say, "Oh my." Instead, smile. See the beauty that God created.

♦ Do something just for you. Take a walk, sit on the porch in the quiet, read for fun, drink coffee from your favorite mug with a special creamer.

SHARE YOUR THOUGHTS: _____

_____

_____

_____

_____

_____

_____

_____

_____

_____

_____

_____

DAY 4

Knitting the Perfect You

For it was You who created my inward parts;
You knit me together in my mother's womb.

Psalm 139:13 (CSB)

Yesterday we talked about our beauty, about being created in God's image. I want to push you a little further here to think about your beauty and what it means to your child. After all, they came from you. God created you, He knitted you together exactly as He wanted you. He did the same for your child. He chose exactly what your child would look like and we need to help our children understand this Biblical truth.

Every time you complain about your nose, your child who has the same nose begins to wonder if her own nose isn't good enough. Each time you say that you hate your curly hair, your curly-haired child wonders if you also hate his curly hair.

Instead of unintentionally leading our children down a path of self-hate, let's lead them to seeing themselves as God's masterpiece. We do this by realizing for ourselves that we were created by God in this specific way on purpose. We do this by taking good care of ourselves and not complaining about but instead appreciating what God made.

Father, thank You for creating me.
Thank You for creating my children.
Help me love myself so that I can teach my
children to love themselves. Help all of us
see ourselves as You see us. Amen.

♦ Today, find a trait you share with your child; it could be eye color, a unique laugh, a positive outlook on life, or even a love for dessert. Point it out to them by saying, "Look! We are alike! Isn't it so neat that God gave us both this beautiful similarity?"

♦ Memorize Psalm 139:13.

SHARE YOUR THOUGHTS: _____

_____

_____

_____

_____

_____

_____

_____

_____

_____

_____

DAY 5

Replenish Your Oxygen

Come to me, all of you who are weary and burdened,
and I will give you rest.

Matthew 11:28 (CSB)

Motherhood can make the even the most energetic people feel weary and burdened. We need to replenish to be our best selves. When flying, the flight attendant always gives clear directions to passengers to put on your own oxygen mask before helping anyone else. "Anyone else" includes your own child. You must put on your own mask before helping your child put their mask on.

To a mom, this sounds absurd! We automatically think to help others first, especially our children. This concept goes directly against our motherly instincts. But there is reason for putting your own mask on first: If you run out of oxygen yourself, you are unable to help anyone else.

In your everyday life, are you giving everyone else oxygen without refreshing yours? Are you so busy caring for your children that you are weary to the point of exhaustion? You cannot be the mother you want to be if you aren't doing what you need to do to take care of yourself.

Father, thank You for being there for me.
Help me remember to fill my cup daily and
come to You for rest. Help me remember that
I must renew myself in You so that I can take
care of my family. Amen.

♦ Today when the weariness sets in, instead of reaching for another cup of coffee, reach for your Bible. Spend some time in the Word and let God give you true rest and renewal.

♦ To "replenish your oxygen," carve out intentional time each day to spend in prayer and Bible reading.

SHARE YOUR THOUGHTS: _____
_____
_____
_____
_____
_____
_____
_____
_____
_____
_____
_____

DAY 6

Thanks for the Same Old, Same Old

First of all, then, I urge that petitions, prayers, intercessions, and thanksgivings be made for everyone.

1 Timothy 2:1 (CSB)

We are called in 1 Timothy to pray and give thanks for everyone, including our families. What better time to pray and give thanks for our family than when we are doing those seemingly mundane tasks! After all, a mom's work is never done! Just as you finish the dishes, it is time to cook dinner. Right after you mop the floor, someone spills something. It seems never-ending.

While motherhood is a beautiful blessing from God, it is also a lot of work. Our days are filled with laundry, dishes, diapers, and tears. Often, this unending work can become mundane. Just the same old, same old.

So how can we find purpose in the everyday and mundane? Use those tasks, those mundane times as prayer prompts.

When I am doing the dreaded dishes, I take that time to pray, thanking God for the food He provided to nourish my family. I even thank Him for the dirty dishes because it means we are blessed to have food to eat and dishes to eat from.

When faced with a mountain of laundry, I use it as a prompt to pray. I thank God for the family who dirtied the clothes, the clothes that we have to wear, and the means we have to clean those clothes.

Using the everyday mundane as prayer prompts makes the tasks at hand have more value.

Father, thank You for the blessings
You have placed in my life. Thank You for
the work You have placed before me. Help
me be grateful and find purpose and blessing
in the work. Amen.

◆ Today, give thanks for each family member as you fold their clothing.

◆ As you cook dinner, pray for good nutrition and health for your family.

SHARE YOUR THOUGHTS: _____

_____

_____

_____

_____

_____

_____

_____

_____

_____

_____

_____

DAY 7

Mission Possible

Then He said to them, "Go into all the world and
preach the gospel to all creation."

Mark 16:15 (CSB)

In Mark 16, Jesus gives the Great Commission. He tells us to go into all the world and preach the Gospel. Many pastors, Bible teachers, and writers interpret this verse to mean that God called us to be missionaries and spread the Gospel to all nations, to the world. But that also includes our neighbors, coworkers, friends, and even our children. We are to reach *our* world for Christ.

Today, let's bring it home. We are missionaries in our own homes, to our own children.

Being a missionary to my children means it is my job to teach them about Christ. I am to teach them about living for God, reading the Bible, and going to church. But I am also to *show* them Christ by my actions, my attitude, and my character.

There are many creative ways to be a missionary to our family and our world. One day, my kids and I ended our homeschool early and drove around neighborhoods in our town. We prayed over different schools, churches, fire stations, and people we passed. It was a wonderful way to cover our town in prayer, teach my kids about praying for others, and lead them by example. Let's embrace our mission field and be the missionaries we are called to be.

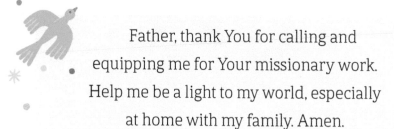

Father, thank You for calling and
equipping me for Your missionary work.
Help me be a light to my world, especially
at home with my family. Amen.

♦ Spend some time today thinking of how you are reaching
your mission field. What are you doing right and what do
you need to change?

♦ Make a plan to teach your kids about Christ through your
actions. Don't be afraid to start small yet dream big.

SHARE YOUR THOUGHTS: _____

_____

_____

_____

_____

_____

_____

_____

_____

_____

_____

_____

Trust the Father

The Lord is my strength and my shield; my heart
trusts in Him, and I am helped. Therefore my heart
celebrates, and I give thanks to Him with my song.

Psalm 28:7 (CSB)

Things happen in this life, especially in motherhood, that can take us by surprise. I found this to be devastatingly true when the doctor told us they didn't catch my daughter's thyroid disease in time and that she could have brain damage. And again, when another doctor said her tumor had grown too quickly and needed to be checked for cancer. And yet again, when another doctor said another of her tumors was showing signs of malignancy. These moments knocked me off my feet and I hit the floor hard. *How could this be? Not my baby girl!*

Each time a horrible surprise shook me to my core, I had to will myself just to breathe. Each time I had to learn all over again to rely on the Lord, my strength. I had to remind myself to trust Him, that He is my strength and shield. No matter the outcome, I had to remember that He is still God. I praise God today because there was no brain damage and the tumors weren't cancerous. But life has brought plenty of bad surprises that have always led me back to God.

Whether your surprises are a health scare for your little one, an unexpected bill you don't know how you'll pay, the loss of a job, the loss of a loved one, a broken relationship, anxiety, or fear, remember that He is your strength and shield and you can always trust in Him.

Father, I thank You that no matter what
comes my way, You are still God and
I can still trust in You. Help me remember
that You are my strength and shield. Amen.

♦ Today, give your burden to God. Stop holding on to it. Give
it to Him and trust.

♦ Write down your burden or prayer request. Place it somewhere that you will see it to pray over the requests. When
God answers, write the answered prayer next to the request
so you can see God working.

SHARE YOUR THOUGHTS: _____

_____

_____

_____

_____

_____

_____

_____

_____

_____

_____

_____

DAY 9

Savor the Status Quo

Jesus Christ is the same yesterday, today, and forever.

Hebrews 13:8 (CSB)

Parenthood is one of the ever-changing things in life. As soon as we find our groove with one stage, our children grow into a new stage and we are thrown for a loop. But it is not just death and taxes you can count on. God, too, doesn't change. He doesn't wear down. He is our solid rock today and always. When life brings change, you can rest in the peace that He is the same.

In 1990, my parents redid the sidewalk at our family home. For fun, my brother, sisters, and I put our handprints in the cement. Thirty years later, they are still there. You can still see 20 small fingers. Each time I am at my parents', I am amazed how the prints have stood the test of time.

Like these prints, Hebrews tells us that Jesus is the same yesterday, today, and forever. He is our stable presence. We can completely count on Him. We can completely count on His Word.

Father, thank You that I can always count on You. I am grateful that You never change, that You are always my solid rock. Help me always lean on You. Amen.

♦ Today, when your schedule changes, when something throws you for a loop, pause and thank God that He is the same.

♦ Read Hebrews 13.

SHARE YOUR THOUGHTS: _____

_____

_____

_____

_____

_____

_____

_____

_____

_____

_____

_____

_____

_____

_____

Use God's Measuring Stick

Summoning His disciples, He said to them, "Truly
I tell you, this poor widow has put more into the
treasury than all the others. For they all gave out of
their surplus, but she out of her poverty has put in
everything she had—all she had to live on."

Mark 12:43–44 (CSB)

The world's view of success is vastly different from God's. The world thinks
we should climb the corporate ladder, have an overflowing bank account,
or win a reality show. But when we look at the story of the widow's mite in
Mark 12, we see that this is not how God feels.

The rich men dropped large sums of money in the offering. But because
they were rich, it wasn't a sacrifice. It wasn't a big deal. Then the widow
walks in with only two tiny coins to her name. She places both in the
offering. She gave all she had. Obviously the rich men gave far more in
monetary value, but Jesus was more impressed and pleased with what the
widow gave.

We need to use God's measuring stick when we are measuring success.
His measuring stick looks at our heart. Instead of being down that you
can't give your family a five-star vacation, be grateful for conversations and
laughter over a board game or campfire. Instead of comparing your child's
accomplishments to those you see on social media, be thankful for the
Fruits of the Spirit you see them living out. Comparing and measuring by
the world's measuring stick brings discontentment, so let's instead use God's
measuring stick.

Father, thank You for the fact that I don't
have to measure up to what the world thinks.
Please help me remember that You help me
have a pure and honest heart. Amen.

◆ Today, lay aside any unrealistic expectations you have
placed on yourself or your kids. Measure yourself, and them,
by God's measuring stick.

◆ Start a habit of seeking God's idea for success before each
thing you do.

SHARE YOUR THOUGHTS: _____

_____

_____

_____

_____

_____

_____

_____

_____

_____

_____

_____

_____

Living the Fruits

But the fruit of the Spirit is love, joy, peace, patience, kindness, goodness, faithfulness, gentleness, and self-control. The law is not against such things.

Galatians 5:22–23 (CSB)

My family loves music, and we love it loud. Anytime we are in the car, the radio is blaring! One day as I was heading out to pick up my daughter from volleyball practice, I felt an urgent call to turn the radio off. I recognized this urgency as God's call to pray. As I began to pray for my family, the Fruits of the Spirit weighed heavily on my heart. I started to pray that God would help me to be a woman, wife, and mom who was strong in the Fruits. Someone who lived out love, joy, peace, patience, kindness, goodness, faithfulness, gentleness, and self-control. Then I prayed that my husband and children would also be enveloped by the Fruits.

Matthew 7 tells us that the world will know us by our Fruits. In the same way, our family will know us by our Fruits. What kind of Fruits are we producing? What kind of Fruits are we teaching our kids?

Father, help me live out the Fruits of the Spirit. Help all nine Fruits be evident in my life. In the same way, help me teach my children how to live out the Fruits. Amen.

Over the next nine days, we will look deeper into each Fruit of the Spirit.

- Make a list of all nine Fruits. Next to each Fruit, write out a way you can teach your kids about that Fruit.

- Read Matthew 7:15–20 and be reminded that a good tree produces good fruit.

SHARE YOUR THOUGHTS: _____

_____

_____

_____

_____

_____

_____

_____

_____

_____

_____

_____

_____

DAY 12

Love: Be Love

Love is patient, love is kind. Love does not envy, is not boastful, is not arrogant, is not rude, is not self-seeking, is not irritable, and does not keep a record of wrongs. Love finds no joy in unrighteousness but rejoices in the truth. It bears all things, believes all things, hopes all things, endures all things.

1 Corinthians 13:4–7 (CSB)

One thing I love to do when reading Scripture is put my own name in the verse. Friend, this practice is painfully eye-opening. Go ahead, give it a try. Reread 1 Corinthians 13:4–7 and substitute your name every time the word "love" is used.

Did you say "ouch" as often as I do? I want to think I am all these things. I want to think I am patient and kind, that I don't envy, am not boastful, arrogant, rude, self-seeking, irritable, and keep no record of wrongs. But that is just not the case. Especially at home.

Why is it that our family gets the worst of us? Our partner gets the exhausted, worn-down wife. Our kids get the irritated, stressed-out mom. Our family sees us when our patience has run out and our kindness tank is depleted.

It doesn't have to be this way! We know from 1 John 4:7 that God is love, so when we ask God into our hearts to be our Lord and Savior, He equips *us* to be love. Pray and ask God to help you truly *be* love.

Father, thank You for always forgiving
me when I mess up. Help me be an example
to my family and the world of Your love.
Help me be patient and kind and all the
things that please You. Amen.

♦ Memorize 1 Corinthians 13:4–7.

♦ Write out 1 Corinthians 13:4–7 and place it in your home
for your family to see. Let these verses be an anthem for
your family.

SHARE YOUR THOUGHTS: _____

_____

_____

_____

_____

_____

_____

_____

_____

_____

_____

_____

Joy: Search for It in Blessings

Now may the God of hope fill you with all joy and
peace as you believe so that you may overflow with
hope by the power of the Holy Spirit.

Romans 15:13 (CSB)

Many people confuse joy with happiness. The two are, in fact, different. Happiness is circumstantial. We are happy when the baby sleeps through the night. We are happy when our spouse brings home a tub of ice cream. We are unhappy if our teen is disrespectful. We are unhappy if one of our kids feels upset about something. If things are going well, we are happy, but if not...

Joy, however, comes from God. He fills us with joy that has nothing to do with our circumstances. When we ask God into our hearts, He fills us with His joy. Even if you have a bad day and are feeling stressed and unhappy, you can still find joy in salvation and God's sweet blessings.

When things are not going well and you are feeling unhappy, pause and begin to think of all the blessings God has given you. When we focus on the blessings, we pull our focus off the problem and find contentment and joy that comes only from God. The sink of dirty dishes can be frustrating, but praise God you have food to eat. The mortgage payment takes a large chunk of your income, but praise God you have a roof over your head. Don't look at the circumstances, don't look at the problem, look for the blessing. That is where you find the joy.

Father, thank You. You are so good to me.
You have blessed me beyond what I can
imagine. Help me remember Your sweet
blessings and find joy in You. Amen.

♦ Write a list of 20 blessings from God. Be specific. Keep your
list handy and add something to it each day.

♦ When you are feeling unhappy, read verses on joy, such as
Psalm 32:11 and Psalm 51:12.

SHARE YOUR THOUGHTS: _____

_____

_____

_____

_____

_____

_____

_____

_____

_____

_____

_____

_____

_____

DAY 14

Peace: God Is Your Kids' Chaperone

Peace I leave with you. My peace I give to you.
I do not give to you as the world gives. Don't let
your heart be troubled or fearful.

John 14:27 (CSB)

When I became a mother, I became a worrier. A serious, hard-core, marathon worrier. Such a worrier that I slept with the baby monitor right next to my ear at the highest volume. That may not sound *that* abnormal, but I didn't just use this monitor when my children were babies. I used a monitor until my youngest was five years old. The children's bedrooms were right next to each other, so I put my monitor right outside the door to catch both rooms.

Then, one day, my baby monitor would not work. I freaked out and decided I would stay awake all night to listen for my kids until I could go to the store the next day for a new monitor.

But I did not need to fear. God reminded me that *He* would be awake with my children (Psalm 121:4) so that I could sleep in peace. Whatever it is you are facing, God is with you. He has gift wrapped peace just for you. Accept His gift and rest easy, friend.

Father, thank You for always being there
and thank You for Your peace.
Help me always trust in You. Amen.

♦ Before bed tonight, or before approaching an unsettling situation, read John 14:27.

♦ If you have a child who struggles with anxiety, help them memorize John 14:27.

SHARE YOUR THOUGHTS: _____

_____

_____

_____

_____

_____

_____

_____

_____

_____

_____

_____

_____

Patience: A Fruit and a Vine

Patience is better than power, and controlling
one's emotions, than capturing a city.

Proverbs 16:32 (CSB)

As a mom, patience can be one of the hardest Fruits of the Spirit. Whether it is waiting for a toddler to stop a tantrum, waiting for an independent child to put their own shoes on, waiting for a child to tell every last teeny-tiny detail of a story, or waiting on a teen to take out the garbage, our patience is tested day after day after day.

When our patience has run its course, we lash out, we say things we shouldn't, we hurt the ones we love. I've seen my children act impatiently toward one another. I am always appalled, embarrassed, and hurt, only to find myself acting the same toward them when I've lost my own grip on patience. We must remember that our kids see us. They see how we respond to situations. They are learning from us.

Patience shows power and "losing it" shows a loss of power. In order to teach your kids to be patient, you need to practice patience yourself. They will see the power and self-control you demonstrate through patience, and want to feel that power in their own lives. Let's pray for patience and practice this wonderful Fruit.

Father, thank You for being patient
with me. Help me practice patience during
trying times. In turn, help me teach my
kids how to respond and react in love
and patience. Amen.

♦ Make a plan. When you normally lose patience, try breathing, praying, and then respond.

♦ Talk to your spouse or a trusted friend. Ask them to hold you accountable when they see you losing your patience. If you need help when they are not around, shoot a text asking for prayer.

SHARE YOUR THOUGHTS: _____

_____

_____

_____

_____

_____

_____

_____

_____

_____

Kindness: A Little Goes a Long Way

And be kind and compassionate to one
another, forgiving one another, just as
God also forgave you in Christ.

Ephesians 4:32 (CSB)

Recently, I was having a hard day. Nothing was going right. *Nothing.* I felt stressed, anxious, rushed; you name the negative emotion, I felt it. As I was driving past a coffee shop, I decided to grab a treat. I *needed* that rich chocolate cake on a stick. As I sat in my car, inching my way up to the drive-through, I just wanted to cry. When I finally reached the window, the clerk handed me the treat and told me that the person in the car before me had paid for my order. This little act of kindness, not the chocolate treat, melted my heart and brought light to my dark day.

We never know what someone is going through. That woman near tears could have just experienced a miscarriage. That elderly gentleman moving slowly could be learning to adjust to a world without his beloved wife. That disrespectful child could be living with abuse. We don't know what situation someone is facing. When we are kind, we may be the only light, *the only Jesus,* they see.

When we are kind to others, we are teaching our children to be kind. When your children watch you react to someone's rudeness with kindness, they are learning to react the same way. When they experience your kindness for themselves, they are learning to be kind as well.

Father, I ask You to help me be kind.
Kind to all I come in contact with, especially
my family. Help my children see kindness
firsthand in our home and learn to be
kind. Amen.

♦ Perform a random act of kindness today.

♦ Practice modeling your manners—"please," "thank
you," "you're welcome"—in all situations, especially the
little things.

SHARE YOUR THOUGHTS: _____

_____

_____

_____

_____

_____

_____

_____

_____

_____

_____

Goodness: Be Good Because He Is Good

For the word of the Lord is right, and all His work is done in truth. He loves righteousness and justice; the earth is full of the goodness of the Lord.

Psalm 33:4–5 (CSB)

Goodness simply means an uprightness of heart and life. God wants our hearts to be pure and committed to Him, and He wants our lives to reflect that. He wants our motherhood to reflect that. To find out how to be committed to God with a pure heart, we need only to open the pages of the Bible. In fact, throughout Scripture, God tells us how to be good. We can see it in the 10 Commandments and the Fruits of the Spirit, just to name a few.

It can be easy to let the busyness of life and motherhood bog us down. I have struggled with insomnia my entire teen and adult life. When sleepless nights weigh me down, I allow stress and anxiety to push out any goodness, and before long, it trickles down to my family. I have to go back and seek God and strive to live with a heart of goodness.

When we live out the Fruit of goodness, we are a walking example for others, our children included, to find God. When we lie, steal, cheat, take God's name in vain, or do anything displeasing to God, we are watering down our witness. Yet, when we are good, we show that God is good.

Father, You are good. Help me live
out the Fruit of goodness and help me
be an example of goodness for my
children to see. Amen.

- Spend some time today thinking how you are showing the goodness of God. How can you improve?

- Find three verses on the goodness of God that encourage you and write them out.

SHARE YOUR THOUGHTS: _____

_____

_____

_____

_____

_____

_____

_____

_____

_____

_____

_____

_____

Faithfulness: You Gotta Have Faith

Moreover it is required in stewards that
one be found faithful.

1 Corinthians 4:2 (NKJV)

God is not looking for perfect people. He knows we are not perfect; after all, He created us. He is, however, looking for faithful people. As His Word says in 1 Corinthians, we are required to be faithful.

God has entrusted each of us with so much: our partners, children, neighbors, church, home, friends, time, gifts. He has given these things to us and desires that we are faithful to each one.

We understand faithfulness in marriage: Don't cheat on your spouse. But how are we faithful in other areas? We can be faithful to the time we have been given by making sure we give time to God each day and making sure we use the remaining time wisely. We can be faithful to our church by attending regularly and serving in ministry. We can be faithful to our home by taking care of it, making sure it is clean and welcoming. And as a mother, we can be faithful to our children by not only taking care of them, but also by praying over them, encouraging them to have a relationship with Jesus, and helping them be their very best.

When we are not faithful, we miss out on blessings God has for us. And, friend, we never want to miss out on the blessing of hearing, "Well done, good and faithful servant" (Matthew 25:23).

Father, thank You for being a faithful God.
Please help me be faithful to You as well as to
everything you have entrusted to me. Amen.

♦ Read the Parable of the Talents in Matthew 25:14–25.

♦ Read the Parable of the Talents to your children and talk to
them about being faithful in taking care of their belongings.

SHARE YOUR THOUGHTS: _____

_____

_____

_____

_____

_____

_____

_____

_____

_____

_____

_____

_____

_____

Gentleness: A Gentle Touch Means So Much

A gentle answer turns away anger, but
a harsh word stirs up wrath.

Proverbs 15:1 (CSB)

The first day we hold our precious babe in our arms, we can't imagine being anything but gentle. Our instincts tell us to use soft, slow movements and to speak in a low, quiet voice. We are tender. We are gentle.

Fast-forward to the "terrible twos," and the gentleness wanes a little. With each progressing year, our gentleness ebbs. We still deeply love our children. But in the face of life, stress, attitudes, sass, and disrespect, our gentleness continues to fade. Before we know it, harsh replies have replaced gentle answers.

Friend, you can still be gentle. When your child has disobeyed for the 10th time today or your teenager disrespects you, you can still reply in a firm, authoritative, yet gentle voice. It takes practice, patience, and a whole lot of Jesus, but you can be gentle and firm at the same time.

When you speak to your partner, boss, friends, and even strangers, let your words be gentle. You are setting an example for your children, and being a witness to the world.

Father, thank You for being a firm but gentle Father. Help me follow in Your example and be a firm but gentle mom in my words and actions. Help my words and voice be gentle to my children, my spouse, and all I speak to. Amen.

♦ Before you speak today, pause and make sure your words and voice are gentle. Remember, you can be firm and gentle at the same time.

♦ When you do use harsh words, actions, or voice, forgive yourself and ask forgiveness of those you spoke harshly to. Even if it's your child.

SHARE YOUR THOUGHTS: _____

_____

_____

_____

_____

_____

_____

_____

_____

_____

Self-Control: Is It Even Possible?

Like a city whose walls are broken through is
a person who lacks self-control.

Proverbs 25:28 (NIV)

Today we finish our exploration of Fruits of the Spirit with self-control. Kids are not born with self-control; it is our duty to model it for them. But it can be such a challenge in the face of temptation.

Let's take, for example, how obsessed I am with ice cream. Chocolate-and-peanut-butter ice cream to be exact. If I didn't practice self-control, I would eat a large—and I mean *large*—bowl of chocolate-and-peanut-butter ice cream seven nights a week. When I do practice self-control, I indulge in a smaller portion only a couple nights a week. This is a better habit for my health and teaches my kids better habits.

Another area where we need to exercise self-control is our phones. Self-control helps us put our phones down and enjoy the beautiful eyes staring up from a nursing newborn, the excitement of a toddler, the giggles of a teenager, or the loving looks from our spouse.

Self-control might sound hard, but with God it is absolutely attainable. Practice self-control in all you do, even in those moments that it seems particularly difficult.

Father, I ask You to help me use self-control in all areas of my life. Help me be a woman of self-control in my words, attitude, actions, home, family, health, and all other areas of life. Thank You. Amen.

♦ Practice self-control. When the chocolate is calling out, when your phone dings loudly, when anger wells up, use this Fruit God has given you.

♦ Review all nine Fruits of the Spirit. Pray over any that you struggle with.

SHARE YOUR THOUGHTS: _____

_____

_____

_____

_____

_____

_____

_____

_____

_____

_____

_____

Lessons from a Crepe Myrtle

Therefore, putting away lying, speak the truth, each
one to his neighbor, because we are members of
one another. Be angry and do not sin. Don't let the
sun go down on your anger, and don't give the
devil an opportunity.

Ephesians 4:25–27 (CSB)

When we moved into our home, there was a mysterious plant in our front yard. After a couple of months, we were excited to see bright pink blooms and discovered it was a crepe myrtle. But the blooms didn't last long at all, and it quickly became quite ugly looking. So my husband decided to get rid of it. He cut it down and dug as much of the root as he could. Still, the next year, we noticed it was trying to grow back. Without meaning to, he had left just enough root that it was able to grow again.

The same happens with sin in our life. If we don't repent our sin, we leave just enough of a root that it will grow once more. Repent doesn't just mean saying you are sorry. It means feeling remorse for what we've done, understanding why it was a sin (go to the Word), asking forgiveness, and turning away from it. Remove any temptation that would cause us to go back. Apologize to anyone we've wronged, and seek accountability if needed. Don't leave any roots that give the devil any opportunity to linger or return.

In the same way, we need to teach our children how to truly repent. When we command our children to say they are sorry without explaining why the offense was wrong, they aren't really learning and will likely repeat the offense. We need to help them understand the difference between the mindless words "I'm sorry" and feeling truly repentant.

Father, thank You for being a loving and forgiving Father. Thank You for forgiving me of all my sin. Please cleanse my heart and help me get rid of any root that may try to grow. Amen.

♦ If you are struggling with an area of sin, make sure you dig that root out and repent. Oftentimes, seeking accountability from a trusted Christian sister helps.

♦ When your child does something wrong, initiate a conversation about getting rid of sin at the root.

SHARE YOUR THOUGHTS: _____

_____

_____

_____

_____

_____

_____

_____

_____

_____

_____

DAY 22

His Power Is Empowering

He made the earth by His power, established the
world by His wisdom, and spread out the heavens
by His understanding.

Jeremiah 10:12 (CSB)

When our family goes on a beach vacation, we always ask for the top floor
so that we can overlook the ocean.

Last summer, there was a tropical storm moving in while we were on
vacation. We decided to stay in our hotel room that night, play card games,
and, of course, eat a ton of food. We opened the balcony door and could see
that it was raining pretty heavily and the wind was strong. One of my kids
decided to look out the main door to our room. Yet with the balcony door
open, no amount of force would open the main door. The wind was just too
strong. Not only that, but the water from the ocean had edged up past the
beach to reach the pool patio.

It instantly reminded us of the power of God. God tells the ocean where
to stop. He tells the tides when to come in and when to go out. And this day,
He let the waters loose!

Amazingly, just hours later when the sun came up, everything was calm
and quiet, and the waters had receded. Our God is powerful. If He can control this expansive water, if He can move the tides at His pleasure, my friend,
He can help you. Whatever it is you are facing in your motherhood, in your
relationships, in your career, in your faith, turn to God.

Father, thank You for Your power and
might. You are amazing and You do amazing
things. I praise You! Help me remember
Your great power. Amen.

♦ Think of a time your problem or circumstance seemed
impossible, but God still worked. Give Him praise.

♦ What is something you can do to remember God's power
and might?

SHARE YOUR THOUGHTS: _____

_____

_____

_____

_____

_____

_____

_____

_____

_____

_____

_____

DAY 23

Discipline versus Punishment

Fathers, don't stir up anger in your children, but bring them up in the training and instruction of the Lord.

Ephesians 6:4 (CSB)

In motherhood we have many jobs. Some pleasant and wonderful, some not so much. Discipline is one of those necessary but not-so-pleasant jobs.

Many parents misinterpret discipline as punishment. Of course, our children need to have consequences when they do wrong, but there are two major differences between punishment and discipline: Discipline applies the Fruits of the Spirit, and it entails discipleship.

First, when we discipline our children, we need to apply those Fruits of the Spirit. We can be firm but kind and gentle. We can give consequences but still show love. We can practice self-control but still get our point across. When we use the Fruits, we are more apt to stay in control of the situation. And we are more likely to make an impact on our children.

To discipline through discipleship, go back to the Word of God and show your child examples through the Bible. Pray with your child and remind them that God forgives when we seek forgiveness. Explain that there are still consequences for our actions, but we will still be forgiven when we repent. God is our loving Father. He is firm and gives us consequences when it is needed, yet He always forgives and loves us.

Remember, discipline without using the Fruits and without discipleship is just a punishment.

Father, thank You for being a loving, fair, and just Father to me. Help me raise my children in the training and instruction of the Lord. Help me discipline through discipleship. Amen.

♦ When you have to correct your child today, take a breath, pray, then discipline through discipleship.

♦ Sometimes we need to cool off before we can discipline our children. If you need a few minutes, take it.

SHARE YOUR THOUGHTS: _____

_____

_____

_____

_____

_____

_____

_____

_____

_____

_____

_____

Mom, Take Two

The steadfast love of the Lord never ceases;
His mercies never come to an end; they are
new every morning; great is your faithfulness.

Lamentations 3:22–23 (CSB)

One day, my husband was at work and I was getting ready for the day.
I turned the hall light on and peeked in the kids' bedrooms to wake them by
whispering, "Good morning." Fifteen minutes later I went to the kids' bedrooms and opened their blinds so the morning light would trickle in. Still
they did not get up. Fifteen minutes later, I went back in and turned their
lamps on and, a little louder, said, "Good morning." Finally, I went back in a
fourth time and made sure they woke up. I was met with great resistance,
and it set my mood on edge.

Breakfast was not a pleasant affair. The children balked at chores. By the
time we needed to start school, all five of us were as cranky and mean as can
be. The day was not going as planned. I decided to take drastic measures.
I sent everyone back to bed. Yes, I did! Not for a nap, but for a reset.

We all spent about thirty minutes in our own rooms in the quiet. Then we
started a *new* morning. What a difference it made!

God offers new mercies, new chances, and fresh starts, too. When we
mess up, when we need a redo, God is there. His mercies never come to an
end. As mothers, we can model Him and His merciful offers of fresh starts.

Father, thank You for new mercies every
day. You are good! Help me offer new
mercies, new chances to my family. Amen.

♦ When your children push you to the limit, offer a restart.
Remember that God gives us new mercies.

♦ Spend time in prayer today thinking of the new mercies
God offers you each day and thanking God for them.

SHARE YOUR THOUGHTS: _____

_____

_____

_____

_____

_____

_____

_____

_____

_____

_____

_____

_____

DAY 25

Kids Need the Bible, Too

Train up a child in the way he should go, and when he
is old he will not depart from it.

Proverbs 22:6 (NKJV)

When I was growing up in the 1980s and 1990s, Sunday school was a vital part of the church. Sunday school was where kids learned Bible stories. We learned about Noah's ark, Daniel and the lion's den, Joseph and the coat of many colors, and so many others.

Now a lot of churches have done away with Sunday school. Children aren't learning Bible stories like they used to. We teach our kids to be good and do good things, and we tell them to live for God, but we aren't teaching them these faithful life lessons through the actual Bible stories. When we teach our children Bible stories, they take the lessons to heart. I taught my kids about Jesus teaching at the temple when He was only 12 years old so my kids learned that even at their young age they could witness. When my kids learned about Daniel and the lion's den, they realized that even when faced with the world questioning their faith, they could still stand strong.

God gave us the Bible and every single story in there. They are as important and relevant today as they always have been. Nothing in the Bible is there by mistake. We need to learn the Bible stories ourselves and teach them to our kids.

Father, thank You for the Bible. Help me develop a love for the entire Bible and intentionally make it a part of my every day. Help me teach my kids Bible stories and help them develop a love for the Word, too. Amen.

♦ Make Bible stories a part of your day by adding them to a homeschool routine, or make them dinner or bedtime stories.

♦ For fun, play charades and get the whole family involved in acting out Bible stories and guessing what they are.

SHARE YOUR THOUGHTS: _____

_____

_____

_____

_____

_____

_____

_____

_____

_____

_____

Hope Springs Eternal

Let us hold on to the confession of our hope without wavering, since He who promised is faithful.

Hebrews 10:23 (CSB)

I love sleeping in on Saturdays. It may be one of my favorite things about weekends. Without fail, Sunday through Friday I am up bright and early, often before the sun, so sleeping in on Saturdays is amazing. No alarm, no schedule.

As a mom of littles, sleeping in on Saturdays doesn't really exist. As a matter of fact, *sleep* hardly exists. When my kids were very small, I lost all hope that I would ever sleep in again. I began to think I was doomed to be tired for the rest of my life.

Then it happened. My kids got older. They started sleeping a little later. And ultimately, sleeping in on Saturdays returned.

When we lose hope, whether it is hope for sleep or hope for an answered prayer, we need to remember that God is a God of hope. He is faithful and just. He sees us and He will be faithful. No matter how tired you may feel at times, my friend, hold on to hope.

Father, thank You for always being faithful.
Help me hold on to hope in all circumstances.
Help me trust that You are good and will take
care of me today and always. Amen.

♦ Grab a sticky note and write out Hebrews 10:23. Place the note somewhere that you are sure to see it multiple times today. Each time you see it, read it out loud.

♦ Text Hebrews 10:23 to another mama who may be struggling today.

SHARE YOUR THOUGHTS: _____

_____

_____

_____

_____

_____

_____

_____

_____

_____

_____

_____

A New Day, A New Gift

This is the day the Lord has made;
let's rejoice and be glad in it.

Psalm 118:24 (CSB)

I just cannot do mornings. Even if I get a full night's sleep, I struggle to get up. Even if there is something great planned for the day, I struggle to get up.

My kids must have inherited this from me because they don't do mornings, either. One morning, I audibly threatened to throw the alarm clock across the room. Yes, I talked to an inanimate object because I am cool like that. God gave me what I like to call a *God spanking*. He reminded me that He gave this new day to me. It was His gift, and when I grumble and complain, it is like I am rejecting His gift. Each day when the sun comes up, it is a gift. When we open our eyes, it is a gift.

To help me remember and appreciate His gift, I memorized Psalm 118:24. I wanted to teach my kids to be thankful for God's gift, too, so it became our morning ritual. Before praying over our breakfast, we recite Psalm 118:24 together. It has become a reminder that the Lord made the day for us and we need to rejoice and be glad for it.

Father, thank You for this new day!
Thank You for each day You give me.
Help me rejoice and be glad in each gift
and help me teach my children that each
day is a gift from You. Amen.

♦ Memorize Psalm 118:24.

♦ If mornings are a struggle for you, try preparing as much as you can the night before. Set the timer on the coffeepot, lay your clothes out, have school and work things by the door. It can make a big difference.

SHARE YOUR THOUGHTS: _____

_____

_____

_____

_____

_____

_____

_____

_____

_____

_____

Say His Name

The name of the Lord is a strong tower;
the righteous run to it and are protected.

Proverbs 18:10 (CSB)

Sometimes when prayer is hard, or doesn't come easily, just saying God's name is enough.

I love going to the women's Bible study at my church; I look forward to it every week, especially because my mom often picks me up and it gives us time together. One day, just after my mom picked me up, my grandfather called. He told us that my grandmother had suffered a seizure and was on her way to the hospital. My heart stopped. Mom quickly turned the car left for the hospital instead of right for the church. When I texted the Bible study leader what happened, she replied, "We will all be praying!" I, on the other hand, couldn't get the words to form.

When we finally made it to the emergency room, my mom went back to see my grandmother while I stayed in the waiting room. I tried praying for God to touch my grandmother's fragile body and bring healing. But the words just would not come. Every time I opened my mouth, the only thing that would come out was the name of Jesus.

Sometimes we go through a tragedy and we just don't know what or how to pray. Sometimes the kids have us so stressed, the prayers just won't come. Friend, know that it's okay. When the words won't come, just say the name of Jesus and trust in Him.

Father, I am so thankful for the power Your
name holds. Help me always remember
that I can say the name of Jesus and You
will be there. Amen.

♦ When struggles and stress in motherhood have you at a
loss for what to pray, when your child is struggling and
you don't know how to help, or when busyness has you
exhausted, just repeat the name of Jesus over and over.

♦ Connect with a sister in Christ. Make a plan for when you
are each struggling. When you need her to pray, text her
asking for prayer, or maybe even use a code word or specific emoji. When she is struggling and texts you, be her
voice and pray for her.

SHARE YOUR THOUGHTS: _____

_____

_____

_____

_____

_____

_____

_____

_____

_____

DAY 29

A Sweet-Smelling Fragrance

For to God we are the fragrance of Christ
among those who are being saved and
among those who are perishing.

2 Corinthians 2:15 (CSB)

The Bible says we are the fragrance of Christ. But what exactly does that mean? Have you ever walked into the kitchen and been smacked in the face with a horrible odor? You immediately start looking for the source of the smell—the garbage, the refrigerator, the sink, the pantry—until you find it. Or have you ever walked into a room and been overcome with how wonderful it smelled? Even then you would seek out the source of the smell. Is something baking? Is there a bouquet of flowers? Is a scented candle burning?

I don't think it is any mistake that the Bible uses the sense of smell, because this sense is so powerful. Our noses constantly pick up smells, some good and some bad, some even bringing up memories from our past. Fragrance can be a powerful thing.

In much the same way, our lives should let off the fragrance of Christ. We are not perfect; we will never be, this side of heaven. But our fragrance, our essence, needs to point others to the One who is perfect. When others, especially our children and our family, are around us, they should be pointed to the Father. Is your fragrance leading your family and others to Christ?

Father, help my life be a sweet-smelling
fragrance that always points others,
especially my children, to You. Amen.

- Memorize 2 Corinthians 2:15.

- Gather some items that smell good and some that
  smell awful. Have your children smell the different items
  and explain how the smells make them feel. Then read
  2 Corinthians 2:15 and explain that we need to be a good
  smell to lead others to Jesus.

SHARE YOUR THOUGHTS: _____

_____

_____

_____

_____

_____

_____

_____

_____

_____

_____

_____

_____

Overworked.
Underappreciated.

Whatever you do, do it from the heart, as something
done for the Lord and not for people.

Colossians 3:23 (CSB)

Our children are the lights of our life, but, if we are being honest, there are
downright hard days. On one of my particularly hard days, tea was spilled
on a floor that was just mopped, fresh laundry was haphazardly tossed into
drawers, folded blankets were thrown back onto the floor, and the dinner
I cooked didn't receive a single word of praise or gratitude. I felt frustrated
and hurt, overworked and underappreciated.

As I got ready for bed that night, I whined to God. *Why don't they care? Why
do they make a mess when I work so hard to clean up? Why don't they appreciate
me? Why don't they say thank you?*

God completely understood. God knows what it feels like to do something for someone and receive no thank-you in return. He knows what it's
like to talk, to pour out His heart, and have no one listen. He gets what it is
like to give His love and not have it reciprocated. Yet, just as we still deeply
love our children, God still deeply loves us. He still reaches out to us and He
still helps us.

Father, thank You for loving me even when
I make a mistake. Help me remember that
even when I am feeling overworked and
underappreciated, You understand me, and
I can turn to You. Amen.

♦ It is easy to get frustrated with our children when they
make a mess or don't pick up after themselves or even
when they fail to use manners. Instead of letting the stress
get to you, use those times as teachable moments. Keep
calm and teach them.

♦ When God blesses you, thank Him. When He helps you,
praise Him. Practice this until it becomes a beautiful and
intentional habit. Lead your children in doing the same,
giving thanks and praising, so that they develop the intentional habit of showing gratitude and appreciation.

SHARE YOUR THOUGHTS: _____

_____

_____

_____

_____

_____

_____

_____

DAY 31

Lean on Jesus

But He said to me, "My grace is sufficient for you, for my power is perfected in weakness."

2 Corinthians 12:9 (CSB)

In other words, lean on Jesus. The world wants moms to think they have to have it all together. Social media and TV throw perfection in our faces day after day. We are led to believe that if we look a certain way, make particular meals, create fun crafts, and have super-achieving kids, we have it made. And when we don't, we feel weak, as if we have failed.

Friend, hear me now: You don't need Pinterest-perfect recipes, a glam makeup look, or an HGTV-worthy house; you need *Jesus*. You need Jesus at 2:00 a.m. when the baby wakes up for the third time. You need Jesus when potty training has gone awry. You need Jesus when the bills total more than your income. You need Jesus when you and your spouse haven't had a date in months. You need Jesus when the teenager is shutting you out. You need Jesus when your baby leaves for college. *You need Jesus.*

Your tears don't mean you are weak, because His grace is sufficient for you. When you are exhausted and crying on the bathroom floor, remember that when you feel weak, He is strong. When you feel like you aren't enough, He is. Lean on Jesus.

Father, thank You for being all that
I need. Thank You for never leaving me.
Lord, help me remember that when I feel
weak or less than, Your grace is enough.
That You are enough. Amen.

♦ Memorize 2 Corinthians 12:19.

♦ The next time you feel weak, acknowledge that His grace
and power are at work and can strengthen you, and give
thanks to God.

SHARE YOUR THOUGHTS: _____

_____

_____

_____

_____

_____

_____

_____

_____

_____

_____

_____

Hello, My Name Is Jenifer and I Am a Yeller

My dear brothers and sisters, understand this:
Everyone should be quick to listen, slow to speak,
and slow to anger.

James 1:19 (CSB)

One day, as I was going about my business, I hit "play" to listen to a cassette tape on my little boom box. What I didn't realize until a few hours later was that when I hit "play," I actually hit "record."

I was so distracted that it actually took a few hours before I realized the music had never played. When I hit "rewind" to "play" it again, to my absolute surprise, music didn't fill my kitchen. I heard an angry, mean woman screaming at my precious kids. *I heard me.*

I never thought I was a yeller until that day. I couldn't believe it was my voice on that tape screaming at my children. As I sat on the floor crying, I begged God to forgive me and help me. A few days later we were having a really rough and upsetting day, but when I opened my mouth to scream, nothing came out. It was like my voice was gone. In that moment, God reminded me of the tape and my prayer.

I'd love to say that I never yelled again, but I would be lying. Many times over the years I have had to go back to God and ask Him yet again to forgive me and help me not to be a yeller. God doesn't want us to be yellers; He wants us to be quick to listen, slow to speak, and slow to anger. But if you are a yeller, God will forgive you and help you.

Father, please forgive me for yelling. Help
me remember that You want me to be slow to
anger and to have my words sweet like honey.
Help me discipline through discipleship
and the Fruits of the Spirit, and correct my
children without yelling. Amen.

♦ Read Proverbs 16:24; it is a great reminder to keep your
words sweet as a honeycomb!

♦ When you feel the urge to yell, stop, take a deep breath,
and ask God to help you. Teach your kids the mantra "Quick
to listen; slow to speak" and explain to them what a valuable tool this is in life.

SHARE YOUR THOUGHTS: _____

_____

_____

_____

_____

_____

_____

_____

_____

DAY 33

Enjoy the Season

There is an occasion for everything, and a time for
every activity under heaven.

Ecclesiastes 3:1 (CSB)

If I had just one piece of advice to share with a new mom, it would be to enjoy the season. As we snuggle our newborn close, we can't wait until they crawl, then we are anxious for their first steps. Soon we look forward to when they are starting school and learning new things. We are excited to watch them on the ball field or at a dance recital. One day we start thinking about when they can take care of themselves. We are constantly thinking about the next season.

As a new mom, I often heard advice like "Don't blink!" and "They grow up too fast, you might miss it!" I ignored those words and found out too late how right they were. I would love so much to once again snuggle in and, as my son always said, rock-a-bye with my babies. Each season is beautiful and worth appreciating at the moment.

Friend, the seasons will change quickly enough. Your child will hit all those milestones before you know it. God tells us in Ecclesiastes that there is a time for every activity. Don't rush it and don't wish the time away. Enjoy the moment God has you in right now.

Father, thank You for each season I get
with my children. You have greatly blessed
me! Help me stop rushing the time and
enjoy my children. Amen.

♦ Read Ecclesiastes 3:1–15.

♦ Intentionally put down your phone for an hour today. Do
something with your kids. Read a book and act it out, do
a puzzle, go on a walk—something to truly enjoy time with
your child.

SHARE YOUR THOUGHTS: _____

_____

_____

_____

_____

_____

_____

_____

_____

_____

_____

_____

Do unto Others

Therefore, whatever you want others to do
for you, do also the same for them, for this is
the Law and the Prophets.

Matthew 7:12 (CSB)

As moms, we often find ourselves telling our kids about the Golden Rule: "Do unto others what you would have them do unto you." The Golden Rule is straight from the Bible. When we tell our children to treat others as they want to be treated, we are teaching them Scripture.

We tell our kids this rule when they won't share a toy or when they take the last cookie or talk disrespectfully. We expect our kids to understand and follow the rule, which is not necessarily about how they *are* being treated, but how they *want* to be treated.

Let's flip the switch. Are we treating our kids the way we want to be treated? When we talk to our kids, we expect them to listen to us. We even want them to make eye contact with us. Yet, do we always give our kids that same respect? Do we put the phone down and make eye contact with them as they speak? We want our kids to honor their parents, but are we careful to honor our spouse? Our kids learn by our example. Are you setting a godly example for your kids to follow? Mama, follow the Golden Rule so that your children have an example to follow.

Father, thank You for setting the very
best examples for me to follow. Help me
be an example worthy of my children to
follow. Amen.

♦ The next time you need to remind your child of the Golden Rule, instead, sit them down and read it straight from the Bible (Matthew 7:12). Then talk about how God wants us to treat others.

♦ Our kids like to have our attention. Practice pausing what you are doing and making eye contact with them as they speak. Not only will it make them feel special, but it will also teach them to do the same.

SHARE YOUR THOUGHTS: _____

_____

_____

_____

_____

_____

_____

_____

_____

_____

DAY 35

The Original Artist

In the beginning God created the
heavens and the earth.

Genesis 1:1 (CSB)

I don't think it is any mistake that the first verses in the Bible are about God's artistry. He is the master artist. He created things we couldn't even imagine on our own. He simply spoke and all the universe appeared. That is power and greatness.

It's easy to marvel at the oceans or mountains when you are on vacation, or admire the 10 fingers and toes of your newborn, but what about the everyday? When the bumblebee that lands on a flower to pollinate its sweet nectar, or the trees that bend in the wind but never break? What about the way the body heals itself after a cut? Or how no two people have the same fingerprints? God did all of it, every tiny, intricate detail.

We live in a very technological world now that keeps our eyes distracted, our minds constantly turning, and pressures us to move from one thing to the next. Our kids especially feel these effects of technology, the pressure to keep up, for the fear of missing out. When we don't take a moment to pause and look up, we risk missing all the beauty and majesty around us. It's okay to put technology away, it's okay to sit and do nothing, it's okay to tell the kids to turn off the TV and go outside, it's okay to just watch the clouds roll by. Friend, learn to appreciate the beauty of God's creation.

Father, thank You for all of Your creation.
Help me keep my eyes open and appreciate
all the beauty You have made. Amen.

♦ Read Genesis 1.

♦ Take the kids on a walk. Not a sweaty power walk, but a creation-appreciating walk. Look for shapes in the clouds, stop and smell the flowers, watch the birds, just enjoy and appreciate God's handiwork.

SHARE YOUR THOUGHTS: _____

_____

_____

_____

_____

_____

_____

_____

_____

_____

_____

_____

_____

Time to Spring Clean

Draw near to God, and He will draw near to you.
Cleanse your hands, sinners, and purify your
hearts, you double-minded.

James 4:8 (CSB)

With each season change, it is the perfect time to do some deep cleaning.
I try to keep up on my home regularly, but every so often it is time to bring
out the big guns, so to speak. Clean the garage, wash the windows, wipe
down the baseboards, clean the carpets—all those big deep-cleaning jobs.

Sometimes we need to do a deep clean of our life, too. We need to
evaluate our priorities and values and go over the things we do, say, and
watch. Are we watching TV shows that are inappropriate? Are we hanging
out with people who are steering us away from Christ? Is our schedule so
overbooked that time with God is being pushed out? We can also do a deep
cleaning with our kids to ensure that they are living healthy and happy lives
and are connected with Christ as they grow. Are we allowing them to watch
shows, listen to music, hang out with friends, and engage in activities that
are setting them up for success?

When we put wedges in between us and God, we push Him further out.
But when we draw near to God, He draws near to us.

Father, thank You for wanting me.
Help me rid my life of anything that puts a
wedge between You and me. Help me rid my
children's lives of anything that will hinder
them from coming closer to You. Amen.

◆ Take some time to sit down and think about your life. Think of the TV shows and movies you watch, the music you listen to, books you read, the people you hang out with. If there is anything that is hindering your walk with God, even in a small way, clean it out.

◆ Also take time to think about your children's lives. Don't let anything in that will keep them from growing closer to God.

SHARE YOUR THOUGHTS: _____

_____

_____

_____

_____

_____

_____

_____

_____

Trust Fall

Trust in the Lord with all your heart, and do not rely on your own understanding; in all your ways know Him, and He will make your paths straight.

Proverbs 3:5–6 (CSB)

When I was a kid, our church had a shelf off the balcony. For some mysterious reason, people tossed things up toward the balcony so that they would land on this shelf. In order to retrieve the keys or toys that found their way up there, my dad would hold one of us by our ankles and carefully lower us down onto the shelf to grab the item.

As a mom now, I can imagine all the moms watching in horror as a young child was dangled by their ankle over a balcony. But Dad was in complete control and none of us kids were afraid. We knew he had a solid grip and wouldn't let us get hurt.

Friend, God has a solid grip. He isn't going to drop you. You may feel a shake. You may feel like you are upside down. You might even hear gasps from the world. But God has you. Whatever you are facing, even when it's something challenging like a rebellious teen or a health issue, God has you. Trust Him with all of your heart.

Father, thank You for being reliable and having a solid grip on me. Help me fully trust You with all of my heart. Help me lean on You. Amen.

- ◆ Spend some time in prayer. Whatever is weighing on your heart, give it to God and trust Him.
- ◆ Memorize Proverbs 3:5–6.

SHARE YOUR THOUGHTS: _____

_____

_____

_____

_____

_____

_____

_____

_____

_____

_____

_____

_____

_____

_____

Don't Lose Yourself

Beloved, I pray that all may go well with you
and that you may be in good health, as it goes
well with your soul.

3 John 1:2 (ESV)

Reading has always been one of my favorite things to do. I read all the Baby-Sitters Club and Sweet Valley High books at least twice. In fifth grade, I came across my mom's Love Comes Softly series by Janette Oke; this is still my favorite book series ever. Reading relaxes me, takes me to a new world, and sparks my own imagination.

Once I became a mother, I didn't have time to read. Or, I *thought* I didn't have time. I was busy caring for little ones, cooking, cleaning, doing the laundry, and everything else that goes with motherhood. But I missed reading, I missed holding a book in my hand and joining the characters in their world for a few minutes each day. One night I picked up a book, and it felt like I was picking up a part of Me again. God wants us to enjoy life. He wants all to go well with us. He wants us to have something that brings a smile to our face.

Perhaps reading isn't your thing and instead you find happiness in exercising, sewing, gardening, painting, doing puzzles, or playing an instrument—whatever it is that you enjoy, do it. It doesn't make you selfish, and it doesn't make you a bad mom. Your children need to see you enjoy life and be happy. While you are being the amazing mom you are, don't lose yourself.

Father, thank You that there are so many
creative things I can do to have enjoyable
moments. Help me rekindle that thing I love
or to find something new. Amen.

♦ Whatever that thing is you love to do, do it today. Even if
you only get 10 minutes before you fall into bed exhausted,
take those 10 minutes.

♦ Spark a conversation with your child today about what they
enjoy doing. Ask questions and take an interest in what
makes them happy, and encourage them to do it.

SHARE YOUR THOUGHTS: _____

_____

_____

_____

_____

_____

_____

_____

_____

_____

_____

Mom, Take Care of Yourself

Don't you know that your body is a temple of the
Holy Spirit who is in you, whom you have from God?
You are not your own, for you were bought at a price.
So glorify God with your body.

1 Corinthians 6:19–20 (CSB)

My son loves LEGOs. One time, he bought a kit to build a LEGO car; he
placed the frame, engine, body, and even the lights exactly how he wanted
them. When he was done, he was so proud of it that instead of tossing it in
the LEGO bucket or throwing it on the floor, he gently placed his creation in
a display case.

Just as my son worked to construct his little masterpiece, God worked
carefully and lovingly to create you. You, my precious friend, are His
workmanship.

One way you can honor God is by taking care of yourself, and teaching
your kids to take care of themselves, physically, emotionally, and spiritually.
Getting enough sleep, drinking enough water, eating nutritious foods, and
taking vitamins are some of the many things that benefit our physical being.
We also need to stay in the Word, talk to a trusted friend or mentor when
we are hurting or struggling, ask for help when needed, and stay active, as
these actions help us take care of ourselves mentally. Not only do we honor
God by taking care of ourselves, but we are better able to take care of our
families and teach our kids valuable lessons for life.

Father, help me honor You by taking care of myself. Help me remember that when I take care of myself physically and mentally, I am better able to take care of my children and I am teaching them important lessons. Amen.

♦ Today, make sure that you drink a few glasses of water.

♦ Take a brisk walk. Even a 10-minute walk each day can do wonders for you physically and mentally.

SHARE YOUR THOUGHTS: _____

_____

_____

_____

_____

_____

_____

_____

_____

_____

_____

_____

_____

_____

Hanging in the Balance

Dishonest scales are detestable to the Lord,
but an accurate weight is His delight.

Proverbs 11:1 (CSB)

How can busy moms in a hectic world keep all their plates spinning in a way that honors God and their family? By finding a strong balance. Moms are known for their incredible balancing acts. We balance kids, work, church, sports, laundry, and dinner. But if we are honest with ourselves, most days our plates are spinning precariously and threatening to come crashing down. We are exhausted and just don't know if we can keep doing it all.

The first step is to pray and ask God for help. The next step is to have an open conversation with your partner. Together, you can decide the best way to move forward. It might be giving your kids more responsibility, like having your teen cook one meal a week or having your littles take over feeding the family pet. You can consider cutting down on screen time, which drains energy and takes away from more important things. And just as important, you can plan fun activities the whole family will enjoy, like a monthly fishing trip or weekly game night. When we have a good balance of all thing things we must do, there is more time for all the fun things we want to do.

Father, I ask You to forgive me for any imbalance my life has had. Help me find a balance that honors you and helps my family be the best that we can be. If I ever need help or need to reevaluate, help me be aware and take the necessary steps. Amen.

◆ Sit down with your planner and pray over it. Ask God to help you navigate all your spinning plates.

◆ Sometimes it is hard for moms to relinquish household duties to children and teens who don't complete the tasks up to our standards. Instead of doing it all on your own, use chores as a learning experience and give everyone age-appropriate ones.

SHARE YOUR THOUGHTS: _____

_____

_____

_____

_____

_____

_____

_____

Connect with Your Child

Behold, children are a heritage from the Lord,
the fruit of the womb a reward.

Psalm 127:3 (ESV)

When my youngest was little, he loved to be right next to me. If I was sitting on the couch, he had to sit on my lap. If we were at the store, he had to be holding my hand. Physical touch made him feel loved and secure. As he grew into a teenager, that changed. He didn't want to be touched anymore, so I had to find a new permissible way to make him feel loved and secure in this new stage of his life.

As moms, we want to show love to our children, but each child receives our love in a different way. In order to connect with our kids, we need to discover *how* they receive love. In his book *The 5 Love Languages*, Dr. Gary Chapman offers a system to help people find their own love language. He talks about each way that people receive love: words of affirmation, acts of service, receiving gifts, quality time, and physical touch. If your child feels the most loved by spending on-on-one time with you, this is going to be how you'll most meaningfully connect with them.

Our children need a little of each love language, but when you focus on expressing your love for them in the language that works best for *them*, your connection will deepen and your relationship will blossom.

Father, thank You for making each of my children different. Help me learn what speaks my love the loudest for each child and help our connection grow and develop into a beautiful and trusting relationship. Amen.

◆ Take the online love languages test (5LoveLanguages.com /quizzes) with your children to find out what their preferred love language is.

◆ After discovering your child's love language, make a plan to do something special for them this week according to their love language.

SHARE YOUR THOUGHTS: _____

_____

_____

_____

_____

_____

_____

_____

_____

_____

_____

DAY 42

Setting the Spiritual Tone of Your Home

Strength and honor are her clothing, and she can
laugh at the time to come.

Proverbs 31:25 (CSB)

To set the spiritual tone for our home, we need to be women of prayer. A friend used to always say, "The mom sets the tone for her home." This is such a true statement! If I am moody, my family feels that tension, and it sets a moody tone for our home. If I am in a silly mood, my family is soon silly and playful. But what about setting a spiritual tone for our home?

We have the ability to set an atmosphere and tone that points our family to Christ. Pray over your spouse, your children, and other requests that arise. Pray with your children before dropping them off at school. Pray when you are driving and see an ambulance heading out on a call. Be a woman of the Word. Read your Bible regularly, and encourage your children in their Bible reading. Have discussions about what everyone is reading in the Word. Be quick to forgive and quick to ask forgiveness. Be a woman striving to live the Fruits of the Spirit. Be a woman who honors her partner and loves her family well. When we do these things, we can look forward to the days to come and laugh with enjoyment knowing we are leading our family to Christ.

Father, thank You for entrusting my family
to me. Help me set a spiritual tone and
atmosphere that honors You and points
my family to You. Amen.

- Today, ask each family member what their favorite Bible verse is. Discuss why they each chose that verse.
- Each morning, pray and ask God to help you set a spiritual tone that leads your family to Him.

SHARE YOUR THOUGHTS: _____

_____

_____

_____

_____

_____

_____

_____

_____

_____

_____

_____

_____

Child Pray

Jesus said, "Leave the little children alone, and don't try to keep them from coming to Me, because the kingdom of heaven belongs to such as these."

Matthew 19:14 (CSB)

I have worked in children's ministry for close to 30 years. In that time, I have heard countless prayers from children of all ages. Prayer is a window into a child's heart. Children will quickly ask prayer for the family pet or a hangnail; the truth is, if your child asked prayer for it, it is important to them and therefore important to God.

We need to teach our children to pray and cultivate their desire to talk to God. The first step is to lead by example and let your children see you praying. Then you need to help your children understand that God loves to hear from His children. When we talk to God, He listens. Let them know that they can pray anytime, anyplace, and about anything. There is no wrong time, location, or topic. Once your children are a bit older, you can teach them the ACTS model for prayer: adoration, confession, thanksgiving, and supplication.

Prayer is simply a conversation with God. When we lead our children to prayer, they will start living a life of prayer that will stick with them.

Father, thank You for listening when I pray. Help me become a woman of prayer and teach my children what it means to pray. Help me cultivate a love for prayer that they will take with them into adulthood. Amen.

♦ To help your child understand that we can pray for anything, when a need arises today—a trip and fall, a headache, an ambulance in route—pause and say a brief prayer.

♦ Don't let yourself get too busy to talk to God. Start and end your day with prayer.

SHARE YOUR THOUGHTS: _____

_____

_____

_____

_____

_____

_____

_____

_____

_____

_____

DAY 44

Church Beyond the Pews

But as for you, continue in what you have learned
and firmly believed. You know those who taught you,
and you know that from infancy you have known the
sacred Scriptures, which are able to give you wisdom
for salvation through faith in Christ Jesus.

2 Timothy 3:14–15 (CSB)

Church is a vital part of the Christian walk, but it is not just something for the building on Sunday morning. I have been attending church since the time I was a toddler. I've always loved church. Yet early on in adulthood, church became more of a routine than anything. Then I realized that church doesn't have to stop when you walk out the door of the building. In fact, you and your children can get more out of church.

Instead of spending the car ride home listening to music or talking about so-and-so's outfit, talk about what you learned. Let each person have a chance to share. For kids, this repetition helps them better remember the lessons they learn, no matter how big or small. For teens and adults, it's an opportunity to share different perspectives and opens up pathways for honest communication. I love hearing my husband and 19-year-old talk about God and the Bible each week as we drive home; the conversations are incredible!

If your child has papers from Sunday school, save them to go over later in the week. (The repetition works wonders.) If you have notes from the sermon, go over them a few days later and see what God has revealed to you since the sermon. If someone was missing from church, lead your family in praying for that person. Lead your family in weekly praying for the pastors.

Father, thank You for allowing us to attend church to learn more about You and experience fellowship with other believers. Help us take our church experiences and bring them into our home. Amen.

♦ Before tucking your kids into bed tonight, ask them to pray for one friend at church.

♦ Pray over your pastor.

SHARE YOUR THOUGHTS: _____

_____

_____

_____

_____

_____

_____

_____

_____

_____

_____

_____

_____

She Struggles, Too

Imitate me, as I also imitate Christ.

1 Corinthians 11:1 (CSB)

We all know that one "perfect" mom. No matter what, she always looks flawless. Stylish outfit, perfect hair, incredible makeup. She is always on time. Her kids look great and are obedient. She volunteers for everything. Her Instagram feed has an impeccable aesthetic. Whenever we see her walk into a room, our heart drops a little because we glance down at our own outfit and sigh, or look over at our disheveled child and groan. We think, "I just want to be more like her."

Instead, be happy for her, pray for her, and imitate Christ.

Friend, she struggles, too. You don't see what goes on behind closed doors. You don't know what her heart is suffering from. She isn't perfect and neither is her life. She may look happy, but she is certainly not perfect.

When we compare ourselves to others, rather than focusing on ourselves and imitating Christ, we are missing out on our own blessings. We even miss out on what could be a beautiful friendship with our "perfect" counterpart. Stop comparing your life to hers, your spouse to hers, and your kids to hers.

Father, thank You for my life. Help me
appreciate all I have and be content with the
sweet blessings You have given me. Help me
imitate You and You alone. Amen.

♦ When you feel the comparison trap closing in, pause and give thanks to God for your blessings.

♦ If you follow any social media accounts that cause you to compare, hit the "unfollow" button today.

SHARE YOUR THOUGHTS: _____

_____

_____

_____

_____

_____

_____

_____

_____

_____

_____

_____

_____

_____

Find Your Mama Team

Iron sharpens iron, and one person sharpens another.

Proverbs 27:17 (CSB)

As a very introverted person, staying home with my husband and kids is my favorite thing to do. I'm not one to make lunch dates or go shopping for fun with friends. And while I always end up having a wonderful time at women's retreats, it takes all my courage and energy just to get there. Yet I have realized that I need other women in my life.

The Bible tells us over and over about the importance of friendship. We need other sisters in Christ to walk beside us. When you are feeling overwhelmed or stressed, you need your team of women to lean on. When you are excited, you need your team to celebrate with you. When you need prayer, you need your team to lift you to Jesus. We aren't meant to walk through this life alone.

If we aren't careful, motherhood can be a lonely job. Even the most introverted moms need community and support. If you don't currently have a mama team, look at women in your church who may be in the same position and band together, or consider starting a Bible study for moms. Start by making connections with other moms and then cultivate those relationships. Having your mama team to walk this journey with you will bless you.

Father, thank you for the team of women You have placed in my life. Help me cultivate those relationships. Help me lift them in prayer regularly and go to them when I need prayer. Help me remember that I don't have to move through this life alone. Amen.

◆ Send a text to your mama team today. Tell them how much you appreciate them and let them know that you are praying for them.

◆ Consider joining or starting a Bible study or prayer group for moms.

SHARE YOUR THOUGHTS: _____

_____

_____

_____

_____

_____

_____

_____

_____

_____

DAY 47

Making Memories

I know that there is nothing better for them
than to rejoice and enjoy the good life.

Ecclesiastes 3:12 (CSB)

My third baby was really attached to her pacifier. Once she hit one year, we tried breaking her of the habit, but nothing was working. We'd take it away, and the very next day, there she was with a pacifier in her mouth! One day, when I was washing her crib sheet and moved the bumper pad, to my amazement, I discovered more than a dozen pink pacifiers tucked in the corner. That stinker! She loved them so much that she had hidden a stash of them to bring herself comfort when she needed it.

Use the same stashing approach for memories. If we tuck them away in our heart, at just the right time, we can recall them and find comfort. We've talked about the changing seasons and how they come and go so quickly; it's important to remember that we need to make the most of each season and create memories to tuck away under our mattresses. Memories help us remember to "rejoice and enjoy the good life."

Instead of pushing the kids out the door to play while you clean, spend some time playing with them. Instead of rushing through the bedtime routine, ignoring the stories you've already heard, or playing on your phone while you nurse a baby, slow down, pay attention, and savor the moments. You will love the memories God is giving you.

Father, thank You for my children! Help me savor every moment with them and make memories that can be tucked away in my heart and theirs. Amen.

◆ Bake a treat with your kids. Don't worry about the mess; just enjoy the time.

◆ Put your phone down and be more present in your kids' lives. Then help your kids engage in life and build memories by offering activities like baking, games, and walks. When they have something to do with the family, they are more likely to turn off the screens.

SHARE YOUR THOUGHTS: _____

_____

_____

_____

_____

_____

_____

_____

_____

_____

Speak Life

Death and life are in the power of the tongue,
and those who love it will eat its fruit.

Proverbs 18:21 (CSB)

If we speak positive words, we bring life. My mamaw would be in the middle of a conversation and suddenly pause for a few seconds. Eventually, I figured out that she was choosing her words carefully. She wanted to make sure she was speaking life. So often, we throw words around without even thinking. Sometimes we instantly regret our words, and other times we don't even realize we've said something negative.

Our words have power. In fact, the Bible says our words can bring life or death. The words we say can cause damage physically, emotionally, and spiritually. Imagine your words are tiny fingers and every time you speak to your child those fingers reach out. Are your words choking your children or caressing them?

The old "sticks and stones" adage rings false. Words do hurt and cannot always be easily forgotten. Choose your words carefully and make sure you are speaking life.

Father, I understand that my words have power. Please help me always choose my words carefully and let my words bring life, love, and encouragement to my children and others around me. Amen.

◆ Take a dry-erase marker or even lipstick and write a note of encouragement on your child's mirror.

◆ Choose your words carefully today. Instead of saying things like "I hate doing the dishes," say, "Thank You, Lord, that we had food." Or instead of saying, "I hate when you don't listen to me," say, "Let's practice listening really hard today."

SHARE YOUR THOUGHTS: _____

_____

_____

_____

_____

_____

_____

_____

_____

_____

_____

DAY 49

Winning the War

For although we live in the flesh, we do not wage war according to the flesh, since the weapons of our warfare are not of the flesh, but are powerful through God for the demolition of strongholds. We demolish arguments and every proud thing that is raised up against the knowledge of God, and we take every thought captive to obey Christ.

2 Corinthians 10:3–5 (CSB)

Friend, I am going to be very honest with you right now. There is a battle going on for your family every single moment of every single day. Satan is after your family. Even when you think things are going great, there is still a battle. The enemy is battling for your kids; he is placing things in their path and whispering lies to them. Sometimes the battles come in the form of anxiety or fear, other times it comes from technology, and at times it comes from lack of self-confidence or peer pressure. No matter what it is, be sure he is working to get your kids.

For this battle, your weapon is prayer.

Just like the Michael W. Smith song says, "This is how I fight my battles." When we are surrounded, and we are surrounded at all times, we must fight our battles with the *only* weapon that works: prayer. When crises arise, we must fight with prayer. When sickness, pain, brokenness, and stress arise, we must fight in prayer. Prayer is what is going to bring peace and comfort to your heart. Prayer is what is going to protect and keep your family.

Father, thank You for continually sending
Your angels to fight for my family.
Help me intentionally and continually
fight for my family in prayer. Amen.

♦ Make a prayer list. Write down each member of your family
and place the list in a place you will see it each day. Then lift
your family in prayer every single day. Ask God for protection
physically, emotionally, and spiritually over your family.

♦ Read Psalm 34:17 and Jeremiah 29:12. These verses remind
us that when we call to God, He listens.

SHARE YOUR THOUGHTS: _____

_____

_____

_____

_____

_____

_____

_____

_____

_____

_____

_____

DAY 50

Team Family

Two are better than one because they have a
good reward for their efforts. For if either falls, his
companion can lift him up; but pity the one who
falls without another to lift him up.

Ecclesiastes 4:9–10 (CSB)

The Bible tells us how important teamwork is in Ecclesiastes when it says simply, "Two are better than one." Teamwork makes everything work better, especially in families; it makes our load lighter, helps others, and teaches valuable, lifelong lessons to kids.

No matter what we do or where we go in life, there will be always be opportunities for teamwork. Our jobs require teamwork. We utilize teamwork in church ministries. We engage in teamwork with our doctors to manage our health. We use teamwork with our kids' schoolteachers to assist in their education. Partnerships, relationships, and marriages require teamwork. Jesus Himself used teamwork: The disciples helped Him spread the Gospel.

We need to teach our family to work as a team and encourage them to continue to do so, day in and day out. It can be hard at times when our kids don't vacuum in perfect lines or load the dishwasher as we would, but sometimes we need to surrender perfection. And we can learn from one another and improve. Let's use Jesus's example and apply teamwork to the family.

Father, thank You for the example You give of teamwork. Help me surrender perfection and teach my kids to work as a team. Please let my family be a functioning team that honors You. Amen.

♦ For a visual, gather some sticks from outside, one for each family member. Bundle the sticks together and ask each family member to try to break the bundle. The task will not be easy. Next, undo the bundle and give each family member one stick. Ask them to break their own stick. As a family, discuss how when we work together as a team, we are stronger.

♦ Include your kids in things like grocery lists, meal preparation, chores, and family decision-making.

SHARE YOUR THOUGHTS: _____

_____

_____

_____

_____

_____

_____

_____

_____

Remembering Your Value

Her children rise up and call her blessed;
her husband also praises her: "Many women
have done noble deeds, but you surpass them all!"

Proverbs 31:28–29 (CSB)

When my babies were young, an older gentleman asked me what I did.
I replied, "I don't work. I am just a mom." This man looked me dead in the
eye and said something that changed my life: "Don't ever say you don't work
and that you're *just* a mom. There is no such thing as just a mom. You are a
mom, and you work hard."

Being a mom is a lot of hard work, early hours, late hours, no pay
raises, no bonus checks, no promotions, and no paid vacations. Your value
isn't determined by a large bank account, business suit, bonus check, or
fancy car. Your value is in who God made you to be. And, friend, He made
you valuable.

Whether you work outside the home or inside the home, you are working and your work is important. *You* are important. What you do matters.
You matter.

Father, thank You for my family and for the value You have placed on me. Help me remember my worth and help me remember that my work is important. Amen.

♦ Reset your mindset to "the work I do is valuable."

♦ Read Proverbs 31.

SHARE YOUR THOUGHTS: _____

_____

_____

_____

_____

_____

_____

_____

_____

_____

_____

_____

_____

_____

_____

Limits Make Us Limitless

Lord, you are my portion and my cup of blessing;
You hold my future. The boundary lines have
fallen for me in pleasant places; indeed, I have a
beautiful inheritance.

Psalm 16:5–6 (CSB)

My kids have always loved to play outside. Bike riding in particular was a favorite pastime. Our kids loved to start at the top of our driveway, race to the bottom, make a loop, and race back to the top.

I always feared they would race too far and end up in the street, so we set a boundary of how far they could ride their bikes. We didn't set this boundary to ruin their fun or cut down on the momentum they could gain; we set this boundary because we love them and want to keep them safe.

God, our loving Father, sets boundaries for us to follow, too; some of His boundaries can be found in the 10 Commandments. He draws these lines not because He is trying to ruin our fun or take away our freedom, but because He so deeply loves us and wants to keep us safe and give us freedom. His boundaries give us hope and a future. His boundaries help us be the best possible version of ourselves that we can be, including the best possible mom.

Father, thank You for loving me enough to give me boundaries. Help me understand why You set boundaries and honor You with obedience. Amen.

♦ Before engaging in an activity, watching a certain movie, or reading a particular book, ask God if it is within His boundaries. Oftentimes, if we go back to the Bible, we find our answer clearly.

♦ Obey the boundaries God has set for you. The more you practice obeying the boundaries, the easier it is and the better example (and boundaries) you can set for your children.

SHARE YOUR THOUGHTS: _____

_____

_____

_____

_____

_____

_____

_____

Are You Brokenhearted? He Is Near.

The Lord is near the brokenhearted;
He saves those crushed in spirit.

Psalm 34:18 (CSB)

If you have faced pain or suffered a broken heart, know the Lord is near. Whether it is the loss of a spouse, grandparent, parent, or friend; struggles with infertility or miscarriage; or even the loss of dreams and plans, friend, He is near. Lean into Him and let Him embrace you.

Last year we had finished our Christmas Eve festivities and went to bed anticipating Christmas morning. At 1:37 a.m. my cell phone rang. *Nothing good ever comes from a phone call after midnight.* It was my mom. She said two words that made my blood run cold: "It's Papa." I jumped out of bed and I threw my shoes on, still in my Christmas pajamas. My husband, son, and I sped to my grandparents' house. As I ran inside, my dad met me at the door, shaking his head. I fell into his arms with the knowledge that life would never be the same.

I am so blessed to have such a large, close-knit family. I spent a lot of time with my grandparents growing up and losing my Papa cut very deeply. Nothing could ease the pain. Tears flowed freely every day for seven months, and they still freely fall often when I think of him. As I grieved, Psalm 34:18 played on repeat in my head. While I was deep in grief, *here He was.* So close. Holding me. Leaning into me. Understanding.

Father, thank You for being near when
I need You most. Thank You for knowing and
understanding my pain. I ask You to bring
comfort and healing. Amen.

♦ Remember the mama team we discussed on Day 46?
When you are struggling with the pain, go to your team.
Ask for prayer.

♦ Memorize Psalm 34:18.

SHARE YOUR THOUGHTS: _____

_____

_____

_____

_____

_____

_____

_____

_____

_____

_____

_____

_____

Whatever It Takes

Then Jesus came with them to a place called
Gethsemane, and He told the disciples,
"Sit here while I go over there and pray."

Matthew 26:36 (CSB)

Make prayer and time with Jesus a priority.

Susanna Wesley, the mother of Charles Wesley (who wrote many of the hymns we sing today), struggled to find her time with Jesus. She had a small house full of children—10 children, to be exact. She loved the Lord and was devoted to spending time in prayer each day. But as you may know, finding alone time to pray with 10 children, or even just one child, is difficult. Susanna was determined to do whatever it took. She informed her children that whenever Mama had her apron over her head, she was praying and should not be disturbed. She would stand in her kitchen each day with her apron tossed back over her head.

Being a mom often means early mornings, busy days, and late nights. We work hard and rarely have down time. When it comes to something as important as prayer, as sitting with Jesus, we need to do whatever it takes.

It will look different for every woman. It will even look different in each season. The key is to just make it happen. Wake up early and take a solitary prayer walk. Let the kids watch a show and sit at the kitchen table for a moment of prayer and peace. Leave for school pickup a little early and stop at the park to pray. There are so many different ways, we just have to get creative sometimes. No matter what it takes, make prayer a priority.

Father, thank You for wanting to spend time with me. Please help me make prayer time a priority and help me do whatever it takes. Amen.

♦ Evaluate how demanding your life is right now. How can you get creative to have some prayer time each day?

♦ Tell your children that when you are praying, you are not to be disturbed unless it is an emergency. Little ones might not fully understand, but have patience and grace.

SHARE YOUR THOUGHTS: _____

_____

_____

_____

_____

_____

_____

_____

_____

_____

_____

_____

Allow Help

You will certainly wear out both yourself and
these people who are with you, because the task
is too heavy for you. You can't do it alone.

Exodus 18:18 (CSB)

I am super picky about how the groceries are put away, so I didn't let the
kids help with this task. My oldest daughter often tried to help put the groceries away and I would have to stop her and remind her that I am so picky,
I'd rather do it myself. Then one day I noticed that she *was* putting them
away exactly how I like. What a relief to know I didn't have to do this task
alone! What a huge help it could have been years ago had I just taken the
time to show the kids how to do it the way I like.

Moses experienced this very same thing. Everyone was coming to
him to learn about God and to be the judge when there was a dispute. His
father-in-law, Jethro, saw this and knew what was going to happen: Moses
was going to exhaust himself. Jethro gave him great advice: Get help! We
can't do it all alone. Not in motherhood. Not in homemaking. Not in ministry. Not in life. We need others to help ease our burden before we simply
exhaust ourselves.

It's okay to get help. Teach your kids from an early age to pick up after
themselves and to pitch in and help in the house. As your kids grow older,
they can take on additional tasks like cooking a meal or mowing the lawn.
Plus, show them that there's no shame in asking for help.

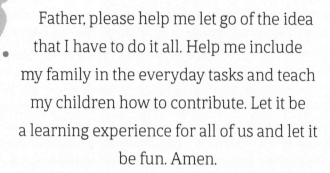

Father, please help me let go of the idea that I have to do it all. Help me include my family in the everyday tasks and teach my children how to contribute. Let it be a learning experience for all of us and let it be fun. Amen.

♦ Read Exodus 18.

♦ Think of a household task that everyone can do together. Set a timer for an appropriate amount of time to complete the task. Once it is done, celebrate with something fun.

SHARE YOUR THOUGHTS: _____

_____

_____

_____

_____

_____

_____

_____

_____

_____

Use the Manual

He answered, "It is written: Man must not live
on bread alone but on every word that comes
from the mouth of God."

Matthew 4:4 (CSB)

We should always turn to God and His Word first. Whether or not life is
going your way, make the Bible your life manual, your instruction guide,
and a regular part of your day.

I remember my very first smartphone. Friend, it took me forever to
figure that little device out! Everything about it was so different from any
phone I had ever had. Somehow, I turned on a safe-driving smart feature
that sent all my calls to voice mail, so I couldn't receive any calls. After a
day and a half of trying to figure out how to turn off the feature and how
to check my voice mail, it dawned on me—I could read the instruction
manual. Aha!

Just as reading the cell phone manual helped me learn my phone's
functions, using the Bible helped when I needed to work on patience
in motherhood and when I needed to teach my kids that their strength
comes from God.

We often go through life trying to figure out what to do. We even go
through parenthood trying to figure out how to raise our children. We try
every possible thing, except reading the manual. Our life manual is the
Bible. Literally everything we need is in the Book. From marriage to motherhood, from anxiety to fear, from illness to broken relationships, the Bible is
a life guide. The Bible teaches us how to parent.

Father, thank You for Your Word.
Each book, chapter, and verse is Your gift to
guide me along in life, even in motherhood.
Help me turn to Your Word each day. Amen.

♦ Read Psalm 119:105 and remember that His Word is
your lamp.

♦ After reading the verse, leave your Bible open where you
read it. Each time you walk by your Bible, reread the verse.

SHARE YOUR THOUGHTS: _____

_____

_____

_____

_____

_____

_____

_____

_____

_____

_____

_____

"Yes" Means "Yes" and "No" Means "No"

But let your "yes" mean "yes," and your "no" mean "no." Anything more than this is from the evil one.

Matthew 5:37 (CSB)

Does this sound familiar: Your teen acts disrespectful so you say they can't go out with their friends this weekend. A day or two later, when they sweetly ask if they can go out to dinner with their friends this weekend, you relent because you're no longer angry about their disrespectful behavior. Punishment over. Your "no" didn't really mean "no."

The Bible has something to say about this. We are told in Matthew to let our "yes" mean "yes" and our "no" mean "no." When we tell our children that they will be punished if they disobey, we need to give the punishment, *and stand by the punishment.* And similarly, when we tell our child we will do something, such as play outside with them or watch a movie with them, we need to follow through.

By letting our "yes" mean "yes" and our "no" mean "no," this teaches our children the importance of obedience and it teaches them that we are a woman, and a mother, of our word.

Father, thank You for teaching me to be a woman of my word by You being a God of Your word. Please help me apply this lesson to my parenting. Help me follow through with what I say I am going to do. Amen.

♦ Before handing out a punishment, stop and think it through. Is this a punishment you can enforce? Do you need to adjust the punishment accordingly?

♦ When your child asks you to do something with them, think before you answer. Don't agree to something if you don't think you can actually follow through.

SHARE YOUR THOUGHTS: _____

_____

_____

_____

_____

_____

_____

_____

_____

_____

_____

They're Always Watching!

Teach them to your children, talking about them
when you sit in your house and when you walk along
the road, when you lie down and when you get up.

Deuteronomy 11:19 (CSB)

Many of us had a role model growing up, someone we looked up to, admired, and respected. I had a wonderful mother and grandmother who taught me to be a godly wife and mom.

Now, as a mom, *you* are that role model. Your kids are watching everything you do. They are learning from you how to be a partner, mom, homemaker, worker, friend, neighbor, servant, citizen, and Christian. They watch how you handle conflict. They notice how you respect your leaders. And they observe how you use your Bible.

Are you being a positive role model? A godly role model? You are teaching your kids much more than the alphabet or how to tie shoes. You are teaching them everything, like how to be a friend, emotionally strong, intellectually curious, spiritually strong, and compassionate. Make sure you are modeling what you truly desire them to grow to be.

Father, thank You for the positive
role models You placed in my life.
Help me be a good, godly role model to
my children. Help me teach them godly ways
to treat others and handle difficult situations.
Help me lead them to You. Amen.

◆ Send a handwritten card to a positive role model in your
life. Thank them for their influence in your life and tell them
you are praying for them.

◆ Make a list of three to five behaviors you want to instill in
your children. Set a plan to model those behaviors.

SHARE YOUR THOUGHTS: _____

_____

_____

_____

_____

_____

_____

_____

_____

_____

Even Jesus Had Family Dinner

So the disciples did as Jesus had directed them
and prepared the Passover. When evening came,
He was reclining at the table with the Twelve.

Matthew 26:19–20 (CSB)

Even Jesus made sure to spend consistent quality time with the family.

Three of my four kids played sports. My sons both played baseball and basketball, and one of my daughters played volleyball and basketball. Watching them play was such a joy, but game nights found us rushing out the door as soon as my husband got home from work and not getting back home until late at night. Then it was showers and bed. This often meant a dinner quickly consumed in the car or absentmindedly eaten at the game.

While it simply had to be this way sometimes because of our schedules, we still strived to have dinner together at the table the majority of the time. Jesus showed us how important family dinner is when he sat down with the disciples for dinner at Passover. The Bible gives other examples of Jesus having dinner, such as at Matthew's house, with Mary and Martha, and feeding the five thousand. It was, and is, a time of coming together and sharing.

Family dinner by definition doesn't have to be fancy. Sometimes we eat a home-cooked meal and sometimes we order pizza. It really doesn't matter what you eat or the plates you eat on; what matters is the time you spend together as a family: The prayer, the conversations, the laughter, and the memories.

Father, thank You for opportunities we have to sit down as a family and enjoy a meal together, even in our busy seasons. Help us make the most of these moments. Amen.

- Make plans to have a sit-down family dinner together at least once a week. It can be as fancy or as simple as you want. Don't stress over it; think of it as time to enjoy yourselves as a family.

- Write out age-appropriate questions for your kids on strips of paper and put them in a jar. During dinner have each family member pick a random question from the jar and go around the table sharing your answers. This is a great way to start a family conversation.

SHARE YOUR THOUGHTS: _____

_____

_____

_____

_____

_____

_____

_____

_____

_____

Who Are You Really?

I will pay attention to the way of integrity.
When will you come to me? I will live with a
heart of integrity in my house.

Psalm 101:2 (CSB)

Picture this: A mom is on the phone talking to a friend, relative, or a sales-person. Her voice is soft and kind. She ends the call by sweetly saying, "Have a wonderful day!" After she hangs up the phone, she turns and shouts at her kids. If you are like me, maybe you can relate to this.

We argue on the way to church and then walk in the door with our "happy mask." We say "amen" to the pastor when they preach how awful gossip is, but will talk about someone in the car on the way home when our kids can overhear us. We act super spiritual and magnanimous at church, but at home our family sees a different person.

Living with godly integrity means we are the same at home, the gro-cery store, work, church, *everywhere*. We cannot talk out of both sides of our mouth. If we claim to be a Christian, to follow God and live for Him, we should strive to live that way at all times, in all ways, in all places, even behind closed doors. This means living fully for God all the time. We become less dependable and less trustworthy when we lose focus on our integrity.

Will we be perfect? Absolutely not. We are human and we mess up. The key is to acknowledge our mistakes, repent, and then apologize to our family. That is how we achieve a heart of integrity.

Father, please forgive me for times I have
not been a woman of integrity. Help me live
a life of godly integrity from this moment
forward. Amen.

♦ Read Proverbs 10:9 and Proverbs 20:7 and remember how important it is to live with integrity.

♦ Think before you speak or act. Ask yourself if this is what you should be saying or doing and if it will it threaten your godly integrity.

SHARE YOUR THOUGHTS: _____

_____

_____

_____

_____

_____

_____

_____

_____

_____

_____

_____

_____

Rip Off the Label

I am sure of this, that He who started a good
work in you will carry it on to completion until
the day of Christ Jesus.

Philippians 1:6 (CSB)

When my kids were playing sports, my husband and I weren't simply Jeremy and Jenifer anymore, we were Lylea's mom or Jeremiah's dad. Sometimes we're assigned labels that we can be proud of, like being known as our children's parents. But other times, labels bind us or imprison us.

When I was a young homeschooled child, grammar wasn't my strong suit. Predicate nominatives, say what? So I went ahead and labeled myself *bad at grammar*. I carried this label well into my adult life. When God called me to start a blog, I actually laughed at Him! Me?! The girl who is horrible at grammar cannot possibly write a blog. But God reminded me that He started a good work in me and will carry it on to completion.

What labels have you burdened yourself with? What labels have others burdened you with? Overweight, people pleaser, disorganized, ugly, insecure, sinner—whatever the label is, rip it off. You are God's and He started a good work in you and He will carry it to completion.

124 ✳ Joyful, Patient, Faithful

Father, thank You that I am who You say I am, not what labels have been placed on me. Help me rip off negative labels and remember that You have started a good work in me and will finish it. Amen.

♦ Write down any negative labels you feel you carry. Then go to the Bible and look up the truth to combat the labels. Write a verse next to each label.

♦ Sit down with your kids and have them name labels they feel are placed on them. Any that have a negative tone, help your children find truth from God about who they really are.

SHARE YOUR THOUGHTS: _____

_____

_____

_____

_____

_____

_____

_____

_____

_____

We Belong to Him

Acknowledge that the Lord is God. He made us, and
we are His—His people, the sheep of His pasture.

Psalm 100:3 (CSB)

Overt symbols of ownership come in many forms. My youngest always
marked his things with his first initial. His toys, books, and countless other
belongings were marked with the letter "Z." When my kids played baseball,
their shirts would have their names and numbers clearly on the back. Their
names confirmed their ownership. We mark our food storage containers
before taking them to a potluck. We mark our Bibles with our names. We
mark the baby's diaper bag before taking it to day care. We very often
mark things, no matter how insignificant or meaningful, to show that they
belong to us.

When we ask Jesus into our heart and make Him the Lord and Savior of
our life, we become His. We belong to Him. The outward showing of this
ownership to Him should come in the form of our actions, our words, our
character, and our integrity. When we live for Him in all we do and say,
when we live out the Fruits of the Spirit and the 10 Commandments, we are
marking His ownership and letting the world know that we belong to Him.

Father, thank You for claiming me.
Thank You for making me new and making
me Yours. Help me live for You so that others
see I belong to You. Amen.

♦ Memorize Psalm 100:3.

♦ Before you act or speak, make sure your actions or words
show that you belong to Jesus.

SHARE YOUR THOUGHTS: _____

_____

_____

_____

_____

_____

_____

_____

_____

_____

_____

_____

_____

_____

Love All Your Neighbors

Love your neighbor as yourself. There is no other command greater than these.

Mark 12:31 (CSB)

"Love your neighbor" isn't just a popular Christian phrase that you've heard over and over; it is a Biblical command. God wants us to love our neighbor. But the question is, who is our neighbor?

Yes, your neighbor is literally the person in the house next to you. Yet, it is also the person next to you at work, the person next to you at church, the person next to you at the ball game, and even the person next to you at the grocery store. Our neighbor is anyone near us at any given time and we are called to love them with the love of Jesus. That means being kind and compassionate. It means helping and caring. It means seeing them as the masterpiece God made them to be.

In addition to loving our neighbors, we need to teach our children to love their neighbors. We need to teach them that their neighbors are the people in their neighborhood, the kids in their classroom, and even the strangers they pass by. We need to help them understand how to be kind and love everyone around them as Jesus loves. We do this by being a living example and helping our children keep rooted in the Bible.

Loving our neighbor isn't a suggestion from God; it is a command. One that makes our world a better place.

Father, thank You for the neighbors
You have placed in my life over time.
Help me love them as You do and show
the love of Jesus to them in my actions
and words. Amen.

♦ Help your children make a batch of cookies and deliver them to your next-door neighbor.

♦ Send a greeting card to someone at your church just to let them know you were thinking about them and praying for them.

SHARE YOUR THOUGHTS: _____

_____

_____

_____

_____

_____

_____

_____

_____

_____

_____

_____

Your Win Is My Win

Everyone should look not to his own interests,
but rather to the interests of others.

Philippians 2:4 (CSB)

I recently watched an inspiring viral video of a track race where a runner unexpectedly helped another runner cross the finish line. The runner in the lead was confused by the race's signage as he got closer to the finish line, so he slowed down and was unsure of what to do or where to go. The runner right behind him could have used this to his benefit—he was in position to take the lead and cross the finish line first—but instead, he put his hand on his opponent's back and led him across the finish line to victory. Wow!

Oftentimes, we judge other moms' parenting choices. We pick a side of the fence on matters such as discipline, screen time, and snack choices, and are appalled when other moms choose to practice parenting on the other side of the fence. How dare she send her children to public school! How dare she feed her children processed foods! Instead of criticizing others, instead of looking out only for our own interests, we should be pushing them along, encouraging them on their own unique journeys.

Motherhood is hard enough without fellow moms giving each other side-eye and muttering snarky comments. We need to look out for one another. We need to have each other's backs. We are all doing our best to be good moms, and we are more likely to make it through the race if we do it together.

Father, thank You for the people in my life
who care about me and push me along.
Help me be that kind of woman to others.
Help me encourage other women and lift
them up. Amen.

◆ Call another mom today and encourage her. Give her a
compliment and tell her that you are praying for her.

◆ Think of a mom who has a different parenting view than
you and send her a card. Let her know that even though
you have different views, you love her and will always be
there to support her.

SHARE YOUR THOUGHTS: _____

_____

_____

_____

_____

_____

_____

_____

_____

_____

DAY 65

God's Protection

But the Lord is faithful; He will strengthen you
and guard you from the evil one.

2 Thessalonians 3:3 (CSB)

I will never forget the day my oldest started kindergarten. Up until that point, my kids had only been with family, trusted church workers, and a couple of close family friends. Now I was thrusting my oldest into a new environment with strangers, a whole new world. I was terrified. We made it through that milestone, but fast-forward to the day she left for college and my husband and I cried buckets of tears. Not only was she once again in a new environment with strangers, but now she was 150 miles away. I was terrified.

On both eventful days, I was praying over her through tears, asking God to protect her, to teach her anything I had failed to teach her, and to be with her when she felt alone. I needed God to be with her, and He reminded me that He would be, that He is faithful and will walk beside her and protect her.

Moving through these motherhood milestones is hard. They pull at our heart like no other. But no matter what we face, even letting our children go to move forward in their own lives, God is faithful. He is with us and He is with them. We have no need to fear or worry. Friend, remember that the Lord is faithful.

Father, thank You for being faithful.
Thank you for strengthening me and
guarding my children. Help me to trust in
You always. Amen.

♦ Memorize 2 Thessalonians 3:3.

♦ Write your concerns down on paper. Beside each concern,
write the words "God is faithful."

SHARE YOUR THOUGHTS: _____

_____

_____

_____

_____

_____

_____

_____

_____

_____

_____

_____

_____

_____

Get Ahold of Yourself

Patience is better than power, and controlling
one's emotions, than capturing a city.

Proverbs 16:32 (CSB)

I am a crier. Not a casual crier but a full-on marathon crier. I cry when I am sad, angry, lonely, tired, scared, happy—you name it. I was once told that I cry too much, so I tried my best to control it. After a few failed attempts to keep my emotions bottled up, though, I realized *it is okay to cry.*

All the emotions we experience were given to us by God. Some of the emotions are good and should be celebrated, and some we need to be mindful of and handle with care. We need to have control over our emotions and be careful to use them in a way that honors God. We need to practice self-control over our emotions. When I was a little girl, I remember my mom telling me that it was okay to be angry, as long as I didn't act in anger. Anger is a normal emotion when things are not going right, but we need to use self-control so that we do not sin in that anger. Crying is okay, too, as long as we are not using it to manipulate others. We need to have a handle on the wide range of our emotions.

As our kids grow, they are going to experience an incalculable number of emotions, especially during their preteen and teenage years. And they are going to have to learn how to navigate these emotions without sinning. We need to be there for our kids and teach them how to use self-control. We need to help them identify their emotional triggers in order to avoid and learn ways to cope with emotions that could overwhelm them. We need to teach them how to talk things out, pray, or sing worship. We need to teach them that emotions are good, as long as we handle them properly.

Father, thank You for creating us with emotions. Please help me handle my emotions in a way that honors You. Help me also teach my children how to handle their emotions in a way that keeps them from sinning. Amen.

◆ If you struggle with negative emotions, such as anger, figure out what your triggers are. Do your best to avoid the triggers. When the triggers are unavoidable and you experience the negative emotion, pause and pray.

◆ If your child is struggling with negative emotions, take them out of the house and have an open discussion about it. Let them know that you are there for them and that when they experience these emotions, they can come to you so that you can pray together.

SHARE YOUR THOUGHTS: _____

_____

_____

_____

_____

_____

_____

Wear Your Armor

Put on the full armor of God so that you can
stand against the schemes of the devil.

Ephesians 6:11 (CSB)

When it came to baseball, my sons all followed in their dad's footsteps and played as catchers. When the boys were playing, we always made sure they wore the full catcher's gear: chest protector, athletic cup, knee guards, shin guards, gloves, and helmet with a face mask. They were never allowed to go out on the field without wearing the works.

The gear didn't make them play better; in fact, it took a bit to get used to playing with it. A catcher wears gear for one reason: protection. And just like a catcher cannot go into a game without gear, we must have our armor to go into our daily battle against the devil.

In Ephesians, Paul tells us to put on the full armor of God and wear our armor for protection against the enemy. We need to put on the belt of truth (knowing God's Word), the breastplate of righteousness (living right with God), the shoes of peace (having peace from God), the shield of faith (faith in God), the helmet of salvation (having a relationship with God), the sword of the Spirit (the Bible and prayer).

We need to put this armor on every single day. And when we put our armor on and teach our kids how to put their armor on, we are better able to fight against the enemy. We are equipped to go into battle.

Father, thank You for Your armor.
Help me put on the armor daily so that
I am ready for the fiery darts the enemy
throws. Help me teach my kids how to put
on their armor. Amen.

◆ Read Ephesians 6.

◆ For a more in-depth study on the armor of God, I recommend Priscilla Shirer's study *Armor of God*.

SHARE YOUR THOUGHTS: _____

_____

_____

_____

_____

_____

_____

_____

_____

_____

_____

_____

_____

Give Credit Where Credit Is Due

Therefore encourage one another and build
each other up as you are already doing.

1 Thessalonians 5:11 (CSB)

The manager made his way over to our table knowing that we wanted to speak with him about our server. He had a look of dread on his face. When he arrived, we told him how *wonderful* the server was! How she was efficient and kind, kept our glasses full, and made sure all was well. The look of shock on his face said it all. Everyone asks for the manager to complain but rarely do people ask for the manager to recognize the good.

Sometimes we do this with our kids, too. We complain when they leave a mess, we punish them for not listening, or we correct them for misusing a word. But how often do we recognize the good they do? How often do we go out of our way to celebrate them for good grades, thank them for doing their chores, or recognize something kind we noticed they did for someone else?

Thankfully, we have a Father who isn't in heaven looking down only to condemn us every time we mess up. God showers us with His love and affection no matter what we do. He corrects us when we need it, and He smiles on us when we do good. Let's smile on our kids for a job well done through our words.

Father, thank You for being a loving and
fair God. Thank You for correcting me when
I need it, but also for smiling down on me
when I do good. Help me recognize the good
in my family and praise them for it. Amen.

♦ Identify something positive and praise your children for
it today.

♦ Do the same for your partner; notice something good and
give praise.

SHARE YOUR THOUGHTS: _____

_____

_____

_____

_____

_____

_____

_____

_____

_____

_____

_____

Quieting the Noise

I am at rest in God alone;
my salvation comes from Him.

Psalm 62:1 (CSB)

Hear God amid the noise.

Noise is something us moms know plenty about. In a house with four kids and multiple dogs, it is rarely quiet. But there's also just noise coming from the world.

Social media, technology, even TV, while they can offer joy and help, produce so much noise in our lives, and even in our hearts. We are constantly flooded with news, information, and entertainment. With so much noise in the world, sometimes it is hard to hear God or even one another. With so much information overload, sometimes it's hard to know what the Truth is. It is okay, good even, to sit in the quiet, to have conversations, to enjoy the song of the bird, or to be bored. Quiet the noise of the world, and enjoy the quiet it gives your soul.

Father, thank You for all the technology and entertainment available to us. Please help me set safe boundaries and know when I've had enough. Help my family connect with You and one another without the noise of the world. Amen.

♦ Plan a social-media- and TV-free day. Instead, do things that connect your family such as going to the park, fishing, playing board games, or baking together.

♦ Turn off all social media notifications on your phone for one week. After the week is up, determine if you really need to turn the notifications back on or if you can do without.

SHARE YOUR THOUGHTS: _____

_____

_____

_____

_____

_____

_____

_____

_____

_____

When Depression Takes Over

You have given me the shield of Your salvation;
Your right hand upholds me, and Your
humility exalts me.

Psalm 18:35 (CSB)

God holds us up, even in our darkest times.

I had always thought depression occurred because someone wasn't surrendering to God. Then, one day, I realized that I was depressed. That even someone like me—who loves Jesus with every fiber of her being, who reads her Bible daily, who attends church faithfully, who has a family whom she loves and loves her, who has so much to be grateful for—can still suffer from depression.

Depression snuck up on me; a broken relationship with someone I love dearly and the loss of my grandfather sent me into a spiral. I still carried on with life as usual, thinking that I was just grieving, but on the inside, I felt like I was dying. It wasn't until I finally opened up to my husband that I was able to feel that God's hand was holding me up.

Sometimes depression is a circumstantial state of being, and sometimes it is a medical condition. Either way, it shakes us to our core. The thing is, depression doesn't just take a toll on us, it takes a toll on our loved ones, too. We can't be what we need to be for our family when we are suffering so deeply. If you suffer with depression, remember that God holds you upright, that you are loved and you are needed.

Father, thank You for holding me up when
I can't hold myself up. Help me see Your hand
in my life. Help me seek the help that I need
and to draw closer to You. Amen.

♦ If you suffer with depression, don't wait to get help. Start by talking to your spouse, pastor, doctor, or a trusted friend today. There is no shame in seeking help from others; it is an act of self-love.

♦ Adults are not the only ones to suffer from depression. Regularly check your children, especially teens, for signs of depression. Keep lines of communication open, and never hesitate to bring it up to a doctor if you see signs.

SHARE YOUR THOUGHTS: _____

_____

_____

_____

_____

_____

_____

_____

_____

Balancing Mary and Martha

The Lord answered her, "Martha, Martha, you are worried and upset about many things, but one thing is necessary. Mary has made the right choice, and it will not be taken away from her."

Luke 10:41–42 (CSB)

When we look at the story of Mary and Martha, we see Martha running herself ragged taking care of the home and the meal while Mary is resting with Jesus. Jesus tells Martha that Mary has made the right choice by being with Jesus. We, too, must take time out to be with Jesus, spend time with our spouse, play with our kids, and relax. Yet, we still need to take care of our homes.

When my kids were little, I spent most days taking care of them and my home. In addition to watching over my babies, I would work on the laundry and other household chores from the time I woke up until the time I went to bed. I felt as though everything had to be "white-glove" perfect at all times.

Eventually I learned that while some jobs must get done, it's okay that not everything gets done. It's okay if there's a load of laundry waiting or the carpet isn't vacuumed every day.

It is important to find a good balance between Mary and Martha. To do this, we need to remember to put God first by spending time with Him. God is the Author of time, and when we give Him time, we find time for everything else that needs to be done.

Father, please help me find a balance that works for our family. Help me remember how important time with You is each and every day, but also make time to care for my home in a way that honors You. Amen.

◆ Read Luke 10:38–42.

◆ Work on establishing a routine that allows time for Bible reading and prayer, family time, and household duties.

SHARE YOUR THOUGHTS: _____

_____

_____

_____

_____

_____

_____

_____

_____

_____

_____

_____

_____

Moms Unite

Therefore I, the prisoner in the Lord, urge you to
walk worthy of the calling you have received, with all
humility and gentleness, with patience, bearing with
one another in love, making every effort to keep the
unity of the Spirit through the bond of peace.

Ephesians 4:1–3 (CSB)

One afternoon, after watching a volleyball game at school, my son Zach
came home very upset because someone had stolen his cell phone. After
some FBI-level investigation, I figured out who had taken it. Sadly, we
learned that the young man who had stolen the phone was also using drugs.
I went to the young man's school, where a police officer helped me get the
phone back and waited for the boy's mom to arrive.

At the police officer's urging, I told this mom that her teenage son had
stolen and was also using drugs. She broke down upon hearing this. She
was hurt, ashamed, and angry. I put myself in her shoes and suddenly felt
my own sense of anger about the situation melt away. Right there in the
parking lot, I asked her if I could pray for her. When she agreed, I reached
for her hand, and she took mine as if it were a life preserver. No longer were
we strangers; we were moms united. Whatever our differences may have
been, we had motherhood in common.

As moms, we need to unite. We need to lift one another up in prayer,
encourage one another, be there for one another, and love one another.
Journeys alone can be hard. Journeys together are blessed.

Father, thank You for the journey of
motherhood. Help me unite forces with other
moms, standing together for the sake of our
children. Help me put differences aside in
order to love and encourage. Amen.

◆ Find a struggling mom, perhaps a neighbor or someone at
your child's school, and add her to your prayer list.

◆ Make a meal for a new mom, single mom, or mom you
know who is struggling.

SHARE YOUR THOUGHTS: _____

_____

_____

_____

_____

_____

_____

_____

_____

_____

_____

Jesus Isn't Lost

Haven't I commanded you: be strong and
courageous? Do not be afraid or discouraged,
for the Lord your God is with you wherever you go.

Joshua 1:9 (CSB)

"Mom, where are my shoes?" "Mom, where is my hat?" "Mom, I can't find my glasses!" "Mom, my phone charger is missing!" I know I cannot be the only mom that hears questions like these a dozen times a day. (A dozen may even be putting it lightly.)

Oftentimes kids assume that if their things aren't right out in the open, they are lost. They don't really look, or they look but not closely enough. They don't lift things or open things. Instead, they turn to Mom, who must know where the item is.

Sometimes, we approach Jesus in the same way. If we don't feel Jesus close, we assume He's moved or He's lost. But He is right there. He hasn't moved or left us, and Jesus is never lost. Friend, He is with you—yesterday, today, and always. Sometimes, we just have to look a little bit harder. Stay strong, stay courageous, and know that you are never alone.

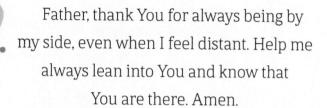

Father, thank You for always being by
my side, even when I feel distant. Help me
always lean into You and know that
You are there. Amen.

♦ A few ways we can see and feel Jesus is to open the pages
of our Bible, sing worship music, and pray. Spend time
doing these things today.

♦ Whenever you feel a distance, don't dwell on it. Pray.

SHARE YOUR THOUGHTS: _____

_____

_____

_____

_____

_____

_____

_____

_____

_____

_____

_____

It Takes Perspective

"For My thoughts are not your thoughts, and your
ways are not My ways." This is the Lord's declaration.
"For as heaven is higher than earth, so My ways
are higher than your ways, and My thoughts
than your thoughts."

Isaiah 55:8–9 (CSB)

I love taking pictures. There is something fun about capturing a moment and saving it, whether it's the image of your precious child's smile or the image of your family on a special vacation. While I enjoy taking pictures, my daughter has a gift for it. Not only does she take incredible pictures of people, but she catches inanimate objects in truly artistic ways. What, from my perspective, looks simply like a children's slide, becomes, through her artistic eye, an image of laughter and joy.

She can see things that I never imagined, at least not until I see the finished product. My perspective of the world around me has limitations, and in the same way, our understanding of our lives has limitations. We cannot see or even imagine what it is that God has planned. He knows the outcome, the finished product. He knows the masterpiece that He set into motion.

No matter what your circumstances may be—trials in motherhood, broken relationships, financial hardships, illness—God sees what is to come. He knows the future and His plans are never to harm you. He wishes only to give you hope and a bright future. Trust that God already knows the finished product and when we live for Him, it will be beautiful.

Father, help me trust in Your thoughts and
Your ways. Help me know that You are always
in control, and even when I cannot see the
finished product, You can. Amen.

♦ Memorize Isaiah 55:8–9.

♦ Gather your kids, grab a camera, and have an impromptu
photo session. Snap pictures of silly faces, tiny toes, and
smiling eyes. Have fun! Notice what each of you sees in the
different pictures.

SHARE YOUR THOUGHTS: _____

_____

_____

_____

_____

_____

_____

_____

_____

_____

_____

Sweep Your Heart

God, create a clean heart for me and
renew a steadfast spirit within me.

Psalm 51:10 (CSB)

At the start of every spring season, I hear the roar of one of my favorite vehicles: the street sweeper. I love when the street sweeper drives through the neighborhood, because the roads always look so much better after they sweep away the dirt, leaves, and trash.

Thankfully, we don't have to wait for a sweeper to come through once a year and clean our hearts. God cleans our hearts from all sin; all we have to do is ask.

Sin is anything that is displeasing to God and anything that goes against His Word. Just because we are "good" doesn't mean there is no sin in our life. When we take His name in vain, when we are discontent with what He has blessed us with, when we have hatred in our heart for another, when we ignore something He has told us to do, when we disrespect our spouse or our parents, when we lie—all of these and more are cause for repentance. When we are frustrated and exhausted in motherhood and resort to anger, yelling, bitterness, and even disconnect from our kids, these, too, are reasons to ask God to clean our hearts.

Whatever sin is lingering in your heart, remember that you can go straight to God and ask for Him to clean your heart and renew a steadfast spirit in you. Don't wait; seek a clean heart now.

Father, I ask You to clean my heart from all unrighteousness. Any sin in my heart, even sin I may not realize is there, bring it to light and forgive me. Help me live for You in all that I do, say, and think. Amen.

♦ Make it a daily practice to examine your heart and ask forgiveness for any sin.

♦ Memorize Psalm 51:10. It is a wonderful and easy verse to memorize.

SHARE YOUR THOUGHTS: _____

_____

_____

_____

_____

_____

_____

_____

_____

_____

_____

_____

_____

Paralyzed by Indecision

The Lord is the one who will go before you.
He will be with you; He will not leave you or
abandon you. Do not be afraid or discouraged.

Deuteronomy 31:8 (CSB)

I am probably the most indecisive person you will ever meet—just ask my husband. I can't choose where to go out to dinner, what to do for vacation, or how to dress for the day. I just cannot do it; I feel frozen by indecision!

As a mom, I have struggled with decisions regarding my kids' health. When is a stomachache just a stomachache and when does it warrant a call to the doctor or trip to the emergency room? Decisions are especially hard when it comes to our children. We don't want to fail. So how can we make good decisions when we are paralyzed with indecision? *Trust in God.*

First and foremost, we need to take our decisions to God in prayer, and trust that He will go before us and be with us. Then we need to have open conversations with our partners. And finally, we need to be open to seeking wise counsel, a trusted friend or mentor who has been in the situation before. Decisions might not always be easy when it comes to our kids, but we can always trust that God is already there and will guide us.

Father, thank You for always going
before me and never leaving me.
Help me remember to turn to You when
I need to make decisions, no matter how
big or small. Amen.

♦ Remember that seeking counsel doesn't make you weak; it makes you wise.

♦ The next time you have to make a decision about your kids, don't panic. Turn to God and pray, talk with your spouse, then seek counsel, if needed.

SHARE YOUR THOUGHTS: _____

_____

_____

_____

_____

_____

_____

_____

_____

_____

_____

DAY 77

Your Child's Personal Trainer

Fathers, don't stir up anger in your children, but bring
them up in the training and instruction of the Lord.

Ephesians 6:4 (CSB)

Personal trainers have an important job. Not only do they help you with workouts, but they teach you what is best for your body. A personal trainer knows that if you use too much weight, you can cause serious injury to your body, and that if you use too little weight, you won't reach your fitness goals. Their job is to instruct you so that you can ultimately do it on your own.

A parent has the same crucial teaching role. We know that if we don't give our children boundaries and rules, they will encounter trouble and consequences. We also know that if we cover them in bubble wrap, they won't learn the life lessons they need to know. As their parents, we need to find a good balance. We need to know when it is time to add more challenges or responsibilities to their plate and when we need to lighten their load. Our job is to instruct our children so that one day they can go out on their own and be not only productive members of society but also people of godly character and integrity.

This is a hard task to carry out as a parent. The key to parenting is to walk the journey with God. We must surround our children in prayer, and we must use God's instruction manual, the Bible, in our journey. When we walk the journey alone, it can be overwhelming. When we walk with God, it can be a blessing.

Father, thank You for my children.
Help me instruct and train my children in
a way that honors You and allows them to
one day be on their own and follow You with
all their heart. Amen.

- Look up five verses on parenting and write them out.
  Proverbs 22:6 and Ephesians 6:4 are a couple of my
  favorites to help you get started. Then pray over them,
  asking God to help you parent in a way that honors Him
  and the Word.

- Plan a screen-free family night. Make homemade pizzas or
  nachos, act out your favorite movies or play a board game,
  or pull out the sleeping bags for a living room campout.

SHARE YOUR THOUGHTS: _____

_____

_____

_____

_____

_____

_____

_____

_____

_____

Are You Full of Praise?

My mouth is full of praise and
honor to You all day long.

Psalm 71:8 (CSB)

While the verse in Psalm 71 is beautiful, it's really those final three words that I keep getting stuck on. *All day long.* It makes me think of how I go about my day. I read my Bible in the morning, read a devotional in the afternoon, and listen to worship music throughout the day. So yes, praise and honor to my God is on my lips. But *all* day long?

When I am frustrated or tired and take it out on my husband, praise and honor to God isn't coming from my mouth. When I get frustrated with my kids for not listening and my voice rises to "angry mommy," praise and honor to God isn't coming from my mouth. When the checkout line at the store is taking forever and I get impatient, praise and honor to God isn't coming from my mouth. So when I compare my day to Psalm 71, I cannot honestly say that praise and honor is coming from my mouth *all* day long.

Still, we need to try our best to let praise and honor be on our lips all day long. But how can we do this? One way that we honor God is to use kind words. We should start looking at others as children of God. When we see others as His children, it is easier to speak kindly. Another way to praise and honor God is to be thankful, in all circumstances and for all things. And finally, we need to worship; it is nearly impossible to be grouchy or complain when we are worshipping God. Let your mouth be full of praise and honor by being kind, being thankful, and worshipping.

Father, You are good and worthy of all my
praise. Help me be full of praise and honor
for You all day long. Amen.

♦ Create a playlist of worship music that you can easily
access and listen to when you need it most. Aim to listen
to worship music of your choice as you go about your
regular activities.

♦ Read Psalm 95:6, a beautiful verse about worship.

SHARE YOUR THOUGHTS: _____

_____

_____

_____

_____

_____

_____

_____

_____

_____

_____

_____

Be Hungry

Blessed are those who hunger and thirst for
righteousness, for they will be filled.

Matthew 5:6 (CSB)

You know when you're driving down the road and suddenly catch a whiff of something delicious? The scent of spicy fajitas from the Mexican restaurant, the garlicky aroma of the Italian restaurant, or the smell of meat from the steakhouse? Suddenly, your stomach is growling with a hunger you didn't even realize you had. And you want food now to satisfy that hunger.

What about when we get a little whiff of God's goodness? Perhaps at Sunday's worship service where the music is incredible, you feel the presence of God, and the pastor's sermon is on point. Then you leave church and the pressures of motherhood and everyday life make you forget all about what you just experienced in the house of the Lord. It is like smelling the delicious restaurant smells and realizing how hungry you are but not eating.

Friends, we need to hunger after God. We need to sniff out His incredible aroma, which is all around us, and let ourselves become so hungry. But we can't stop there. We must pull up to the table and satisfy this hunger that we've built up by eating and drinking in His goodness. We need to feast on His Word, His goodness, His joy. Don't let His goodness be reserved for the church or Bible study. Carry it with you all day, everywhere you go. Be hungry for it.

Father, help me hunger and thirst after You. Help me recognize that I need You and to always run to You. Help me stay hungry for more of You. Amen.

♦ Read one chapter of Proverbs today. Proverbs is a beautiful book with much wisdom for living a Christian life.

♦ If weather permits, plan a family picnic: Go to the park or even just the front yard. If the weather does not permit, spread a blanket on the living room floor and picnic inside! During the picnic, discuss hungering for God.

SHARE YOUR THOUGHTS: _____

_____

_____

_____

_____

_____

_____

_____

_____

_____

_____

_____

Getting There, but Not Quite There Yet

For all have sinned and fall short of the glory of God.

Romans 3:23 (CSB)

Nothing blesses my mama heart more than to see one of my kids "get it" about the glory of God. When I see my children reading their Bibles, raising their hands in worship at church, or having conversations about God, I melt into a puddle of happiness!

Then, just minutes later, there they are fighting with their siblings, lying about something, or disrespecting me. I just want to scream at them, "Weren't you just reading your Bible like five seconds ago? Didn't you just have this huge spiritual breakthrough? Why are you acting like this?!"

Maybe God feels that way about me, too. I can have a spiritual breakthrough, then minutes later I have an attitude with my husband or use my "mean mama" voice. Does God think, "Didn't you just have this breakthrough? Why are you acting like this yet again?!"

Yes, when we have these breakthroughs, we need to learn and grow from them. But God knows a spiritual breakthrough doesn't equal perfection. Just as I can have a breakthrough or a passionate quiet time with Him in the morning and then do something wrong in the afternoon, my kids are the same. They are still humans. Thankfully, we have this amazing thing called grace. When we sin, all we have to do is ask God to forgive us and strive to do better the next time.

Father, thank You for always loving
and accepting me, even when I mess up.
Thank You for Your grace. Please help me
remember that just as I am not perfect,
neither are my children. Help me extend
the grace You offer me. Amen.

◆ Memorize Romans 3:23.

◆ Be careful to offer your children grace, just as God offers you grace.

SHARE YOUR THOUGHTS: _____

_____

_____

_____

_____

_____

_____

_____

_____

_____

_____

Tune In to the Right Voice

My sheep hear My voice, I know them,
and they follow Me.

John 10:27 (CSB)

My daughter recently discovered that the GPS app on my phone has an option that lets you change the voice from the regular, robotic GPS voice to different characters. We played around with it and had Lightning McQueen, Buzz Lightyear, and Mr. T tell us how to get to our destination!

Our children have a final destination: heaven. And along the way, all throughout their lives, they are going to hear so many different voices on their GPS. Voices of friends, coaches, teachers, neighbors, bosses, strangers, celebrities, and pastors. It is our job to teach our kids to hear the right voice, the voice of God.

We identified the different voices on the GPS app because we had heard the voices so often. The more we hear a voice, the easier it is to recognize who it is coming from because it becomes familiar. We learn the voice of God by knowing His Word. The more we read and study the Bible, the more we know the heart of God, which helps us align His voice with His Word. We also learn the voice of God by praying and spending time listening for Him. The more we read the Bible and pray, and teach our children to do the same, the better we will all be at listening for the right voice.

Father, thank You for continually speaking to Your children. Help me learn to hear Your voice and to teach my children to listen for Your voice. Amen.

♦ Play a game. If your children are young, let each child pick a character and not tell anyone who it is. Have them talk like their character and see if anyone can guess who it is.

♦ If your children are older, start a conversation with them about hearing the voice of God.

SHARE YOUR THOUGHTS: _____

_____

_____

_____

_____

_____

_____

_____

_____

_____

_____

_____

DAY 82

Don't Just Phone It In

Therefore, since we also have such a large cloud of witnesses surrounding us, let us lay aside every hindrance and the sin that so easily ensnares us. Let us run with endurance the race that lies before us.

Hebrews 12:1 (CSB)

We need to live with strength, intention, and endurance. Having endurance doesn't mean just getting through something by phoning it in; it means completing our callings with intention.

Every year, I plan and work hard at preparing our family for homeschool. We homeschool intentionally. We strive to follow our planned schedule and stick to our lessons while still enjoying some of the flexibility of home-school. Then someone, a stranger who doesn't believe in homeschool, one of my kids having a bad day, and sometimes even my own insecurity, gives me pause. I begin to think, *What am I even doing here? Can I really teach my kids? Am I failing them?* These questions, and resulting insecurity, cause me to stop homeschooling intentionally and start homeschooling just to get through it.

When doubts or fatigue set in, we find that we quit living intentionally and start living to get by. We start thinking that if we can just make it to the weekend, to vacation, if we can just survive, it will all be okay. Friend, we weren't called just to survive; we were called to run with endurance. Whether you are homeschooling, witnessing, or whatever it is you face, do it with intention. Don't feel discouraged if it doesn't happen the first time; sometimes it takes multiple tries, extra work, and effort. Run your race with endurance.

Father, please forgive me for the moments
I live to just get by. Help me run my race with
endurance and live with intention. Amen.

♦ Go on a prayer walk today. Enjoy time outside in the fresh
 air as you talk to God.

♦ Read Hebrews 12.

SHARE YOUR THOUGHTS: _____

_____

_____

_____

_____

_____

_____

_____

_____

_____

_____

_____

_____

_____

DAY 83

Keeper of the Home

Then they can urge the younger women to love their husbands and children, to be self-controlled and pure, to be busy at home, to be kind.

Titus 2:4–5 (CSB)

Moms come in all forms. Young moms, women who become moms later in life, moms who work outside the home, moms who stay home all day, partnered moms, single or widowed moms, moms to one child, moms to multiple children. But one thing remains the same: We are *all* keepers of our home.

As keeper of the home, we have a big job; the Bible says to be busy at home. This doesn't mean not to rest or relax, but we do need to keep our home in order, to keep peace; to be the guard of our home, to keep the enemy out; to monitor the influences in our home, to make it a safe haven; to make our home comfortable, a place where we all want to be and relax. And finally, as keeper, we need to make our home a place where our family feels God, where we make prayer, Bible reading, and conversations about God commonplace.

This commissioning is a blessed and honorable position. We are caring for the home and family God has gifted to us. This is something we need to take seriously and work intentionally to do.

Father, thank You for the gift of my family and home. Help me be a keeper of my home in a way that honors You and brings glory to Your name. Amen.

♦ Reflect on your plan for caring for your home. Every keeper of the home has a different plan that works best for her. Find what works for you. Having a cleaning schedule and meal plan is often a big help.

♦ Read Titus 2.

SHARE YOUR THOUGHTS: _____

_____

_____

_____

_____

_____

_____

_____

_____

_____

_____

_____

Exercise Your
Spiritual Muscles

But have nothing to do with pointless and silly myths.
Rather, train yourself in godliness. For the training
of the body has limited benefit, but godliness is
beneficial in every way, since it holds promise for the
present life and also for the life to come.

1 Timothy 4:7–8 (CSB)

In his mid-teen years, my son decided he wanted to start working out. Not a lose-weight type of workout, but a weight-training workout. He did research, set a schedule, made a plan, and got busy. The more he did it, the stronger he became. He soon became one of the heaviest lifters at the gym.

We need follow the same approach when it comes to our spiritual workouts. We need to make the choice to grow closer to God, research His Word, set a schedule for prayer and Bible reading, make a plan, and do it. The more we exercise our spiritual muscles, the stronger they, and we, get.

Even if we devote ourselves to this practice, it doesn't mean we have "arrived" and will have perfect days from there on out. It is a journey; just as a weight lifter presses on, pushes through the hard parts, and grows, when we press on and push through the hard parts, we will continue to grow in Jesus.

Father, help me exercise my spiritual
muscles. Help me make a plan and execute
that plan so that I can become stronger in
You. Amen.

♦ As moms, we are our kids' spiritual trainer. Make a plan to
incorporate prayer and Bible reading as a family into your
day. It's okay if you start small. Try just one verse a day; read
together, then pray.

♦ Just as going to the gym with a friend helps hold us
accountable, having an accountability partner helps us stay
on track with our Bible reading. Pray and ask God to send
you an accountability partner, someone who will keep you
on track, who will encourage you and give you a push when
you need it.

SHARE YOUR THOUGHTS: _____

_____

_____

_____

_____

_____

_____

_____

_____

His Faithful Love

Let me experience Your faithful love in the morning,
for I trust in You. Reveal to me the way
I should go because I appeal to You.

Psalm 143:8 (CSB)

King David experienced many difficult things throughout his life. Through these trials, one lesson he learned was to trust in the Lord. No matter how dark the world got, no matter how bleak things looked, he knew that God was his shield and his protector. He knew God was by his side and would always be faithful.

We can have that same confidence in the Lord, even on those hard mom days. When potty training just isn't happening, when the baby hasn't slept through the night ever, when your child's best friend moves away, when your teenager is facing peer pressure—friend, I could go on and on about the many hardships we can face as moms. But the bottom line is this: God is faithful. We can fully and completely trust in Him.

God is there. When challenges arise, He is right there beside you. He loves you and His love is faithful. Turn to Him, lean into Him, trust Him.

Father, thank You for always being there.
Life is so hard sometimes and I don't always
handle it right. I appeal to You. Let me
experience Your faithful love today. Let
me feel You. Amen.

♦ Read Psalm 143.

♦ Play your worship playlist today and spend time in His presence. Let God hold you.

SHARE YOUR THOUGHTS: _____

_____

_____

_____

_____

_____

_____

_____

_____

_____

_____

_____

_____

_____

Give Him a Call

Deeply hurt, Hannah prayed to the Lord
and wept with many tears.

1 Samuel 1:10 (CSB)

It was icy and dark out, but I needed to get the garbage cans to the curb for trash day. I started the careful trek down our slippery driveway, only to not-so-gracefully skate my way down the driveway and land with a painful thud. As I lay there sore and bruised, I cried out for my husband, kids, neighbor—anyone to come and help me into the house. After a while with no help, I crawled my way into the house, into my bedroom, and onto my bed, where I cried from the pain. Then I heard God call out, "You called on everyone except Me."

Hannah was in a similar situation where she needed help. She deeply wanted to have a child, yet every month went by and there was no baby. Hannah was deeply hurt, but she knew where to turn. She went to the Lord.

In times of trouble, it is God we should turn to. Yes, God may not always answer our prayer in the way or with the timing that we want. But when we call out to Him in faith, we can hold on to the faith and trust that He is working on our behalf. Whatever you are facing, call on the Lord.

Father, thank You for always listening to my
prayer. Help me always remember to call on
Your name and to have faith. Amen.

♦ Read Psalm 116, which reminds us that God is listening.

♦ Whatever you are facing, commit to giving it to the Lord
and having faith.

SHARE YOUR THOUGHTS: _____

_____

_____

_____

_____

_____

_____

_____

_____

_____

_____

_____

_____

_____

Guilt-Free

Therefore, there is now no condemnation
for those in Christ Jesus.

Romans 8:1 (CSB)

As women, we struggle with guilt all the time. Guilt from sinful behaviors, guilt from things we could have done better, even guilt from receiving a blessing when others need one. As moms, the guilt tends to pile on thicker. Not only do we have "normal" guilt, but we also have the very particular guilt of wanting a night off from our kids, for leaving our kids for a night out, for spending money on ourselves, for losing our temper with the kids—so much guilt.

If you struggle with guilt, you are absolutely not alone. What's difficult is when guilt brings shame, which can make it hard to focus on the good. It becomes hard to praise God for His blessings. It becomes hard to understand that it is not only good but important to take care of ourselves. And it becomes difficult to remember that we are forgiven and loved.

The thing is, friend, God doesn't guilt us. If your guilt is from sinful behavior, repent. Once you have repented, God doesn't bring it up over and over; you are forgiven. Any guilt you feel comes directly from the enemy. Satan lies and tells us that we should feel guilty. He whispers in our ear that we don't deserve forgiveness or a night out or a new outfit. Free yourself from guilt today.

Father, I ask You to forgive me of all my sins. Help me turn away from sinful behavior and live fully for You. Help me remember that You do not guilt me and I can be free of any feelings of guilt today. Amen.

◆ Memorize Romans 8:1.

◆ When feelings of guilt creep in, ask yourself if it is guilt from unconfessed sin. If the answer is "yes," pray and ask God to forgive you and help you turn away from the sin. If the answer is "no," tell the enemy to leave you alone!

SHARE YOUR THOUGHTS: _____

_____

_____

_____

_____

_____

_____

_____

_____

_____

Our Teacher

You call me Teacher and Lord—and you are
speaking rightly, since that is what I am.

John 13:13 (CSB)

Have you ever looked at the directions on the box of brownie mix, felt prepared to bake, thrown the box away, and then have to dig it out of the garbage can because you quickly forgot the steps? I know I can't be the only one! I do things like this far too often. I read the directions to something and think, "Okay! I got it!" only to have to revisit the instructions over and over because I do not in fact have it.

I've had similar experiences with my kids. I have taught them how to do a math problem or spell a word, only to have to teach them the exact same thing many more times.

Jesus, our great Teacher, gives us directions. Our directions come straight from the Bible. Sometimes we think we have it and ignore the instruction manual (the Bible). Sometimes we think things are moving too slowly and we want to speed up the process or we think we know better than God what we need. But He is our Teacher. He gives us the directions we need to stay on the path He has laid out for us. A path that brings us hope and a future. Trust the Teacher, trust His directions, trust His timing, and trust His plan.

Father, thank You for Your Word. Help me
follow Your Word and trust Your timing and
Your plan. Help me remember that You have
my best in mind. Amen.

♦ Start a conversation with your children today about their
favorite Bible story. Ask what lessons they have learned
from the story.

♦ Spend some time in worship today.

SHARE YOUR THOUGHTS: _____

_____

_____

_____

_____

_____

_____

_____

_____

_____

_____

_____

Ordinary Is Extraordinary

Give thanks in everything; for this is
God's will for you in Christ Jesus.

1 Thessalonians 5:18 (CSB)

We should learn to appreciate the ordinary. Every day that my husband walks through the door from a day of work he asks how my day was. Every day my answer is the same: "It was just a day." Nothing exciting. Nothing new. Nothing special. When the kids were little, it was diapers, nursing, laundry, dusting, vacuuming, scrubbing, and cooking. As the kids got older, the days were marked by homeschool, laundry, dusting, vacuuming, scrubbing, cooking, and sports. But my husband always reminds me that there is nothing wrong with having "just a day."

As moms, our days often look the same. Nothing changes. There is nothing special. We get excited because we used a brand-new mop or put new windshield wipers on the car. The ordinary can be boring, even frustrating, at times. But, friend, the ordinary is okay.

God is a God of ordinary. Jesus wasn't born in a fancy palace; he was born in a stable. He didn't ride into town in a fancy chariot; he rode into town on a donkey. God is a God of the everyday, the ordinary, the mundane. Your ordinary day is okay! Don't let lust for sparkle and newness draw you away from what God has in store for you. Enjoy your ordinary. Appreciate your ordinary. Love your ordinary.

Father, thank You for all my blessings!
You are so good. Help me remember that
You are a God of the ordinary and You are
in my ordinary. Thank You, Lord! Amen.

♦ Write a list of 15 everyday, ordinary things you are thankful for. Add something new to this gratitude list each day this week.

♦ Just as a pinch of salt gives food a little flavor or creamer gives your coffee a little something special, add a little something extraordinary to your day. Maybe it's lighting a scented candle you love, reading a chapter of your favorite book, or wearing your favorite necklace. Even these little things can make the day special.

SHARE YOUR THOUGHTS: _____

_____

_____

_____

_____

_____

_____

_____

_____

_____

Mama Needs ~~Coffee~~
~~Chocolate~~ ~~Wine~~ Jesus

And my God will supply all your needs according to
His riches in glory in Christ Jesus.

Philippians 4:19 (CSB)

We live in a culture that encourages people to turn to indulgences when
they have a tough day with the kids or when life feels even the slightest bit
hard. Tired? Drink more coffee. Sad? Eat some chocolate. Frustrated? Grab
a bottle of wine. Just look at all the T-shirts, throw pillows, and dish towels
that have sayings like "Mama needs wine" and "But first, coffee!" And the
social media posts that say things like "Mama needs wine because my kids
whine," or a picture of a coffee with the caption "Working on my fifth cup
because, kids." Even if we are feeling grounded and positive, we still often
feel tempted to turn to these things to celebrate.

Friends, we don't need coffee, chocolate, or wine when we feel lost or
run-down (or feel like celebrating). God fulfills all our needs according to
His riches in glory in Christ Jesus. When life is hard, we need to turn to God.
When things are not going well—the kids are acting out, you are fighting with
your spouse—turn to God. Nothing else, absolutely nothing else, is going to
help you in the way that you truly need to be helped. When things are going
well, when we are happy, when we want to celebrate, we also need to turn to
God. We should give praise to Him and thank Him for His blessings.

Chocolate, coffee, and wine are not bad in and of themselves. But we need
to be women who turn to God in the bad times and praise Him in the good
times. Friend, when you need that break, reach for Jesus. He is all you need.

Father, thank You for being all that I need!
Help me to remember to thank You and
praise You in the good times and turn to
You for help and comfort in the bad times.
You are so good, and I praise You! Amen.

♦ When life gets hard today or you start to feel exhausted,
instead of reaching for another cup of coffee or a cookie,
reach out to Jesus. Pray and spend a few minutes reading
the Bible.

♦ Memorize Philippians 4:19.

SHARE YOUR THOUGHTS: _____

_____

_____

_____

_____

_____

_____

_____

_____

_____

_____

CONCLUSION

Friend,

Thank you for spending the past 90 days with me! My hope is that you have felt encouraged and inspired and have found a way to spend intentional time with Jesus each day. Even when it is hard, even if you feel you don't have the time, make time to be with Him and know that it is good.

As you come away from this book of devotions, I want you to remember a few things. Remember that you are not alone on this journey. We have all been through the hard days and have all worried that we are failing as moms at some point. Remember that you are special and loved. God created you on purpose and for a purpose, and He loves you deeply. Remember that you are beautiful exactly the way you are right now, during 2:00 a.m. feeding sessions, when you're in the school drop-off line, when you're at the grocery store, right before bed, and when you wake up. You are beautiful. And finally, remember that you are doing a good job. Being a mom is hard and we will never be perfect, but you are doing a good job. Keep up the good work, friend.

May I pray for you?

Father, thank You for this dear friend. As she navigates motherhood, I pray that You would touch her. Let her feel Your love. Help her be drawn to You and the Bible each day. Let prayer and Bible reading become not just a daily habit, but a deep-rooted desire in her heart. I pray that You would bless her and her family. Amen.

Sweet blessings,
Jenifer

REFERENCES

Chapman, Gary. *The 5 Love Languages*. Chicago: Northfield Publishing, 2015. 5LoveLanguages.com.

Shirer, Priscilla. *The Armor of God*. Nashville: LifeWay Press, 2015.

Smith, Michael W. "Surrounded (Fight My Battles)." Track 8 on *Surrounded*. Rocketown Records/The Fuel Music, 2018, compact disc.

ACKNOWLEDGMENTS

I would like to thank my family for their endless love and support throughout this process. Thank you for standing by my side, encouraging me, and praying for me.

I would also like to thank the team at Callisto for your faith in me and for this opportunity. Special thanks to Sean Newcott for working so closely with me to help this devotional be what it is.

ABOUT THE AUTHOR

Jenifer Metzger is the founder and co-leader of Woman to Woman Ministries. She has a passion for ministering to women and encouraging women. Jenifer and her husband, Jeremy, have been married 23 years. Together they have four incredible children, one fantastic son-in-law, one wonderful daughter-in-law, and one perfect grandson. She calls her family her blessings from heaven. Jenifer loves serving alongside her husband in ministry. She is learning to say "yes" to God and loves the journey He is taking her on. She blogs for Woman to Woman Ministries at W2WMinistries.org, as well as at her own blog, JeniferMetzger.org.

CPSIA information can be obtained
at www.ICGtesting.com
Printed in the USA
JSHW051630090221
11688JS00005B/14